When We Are Seen

When We Are Seen

How to Come into Your Power—and Empower Others Along the Way

Denise Young

CROWN
NEW YORK

Copyright © 2024 by Denise Young

Published in the United States by Crown, an imprint
of the Crown Publishing Group, a division of
Penguin Random House LLC, New York.
crownpublishing.com

CROWN and the Crown colophon are registered
trademarks of Penguin Random House LLC.

Library of Congress Cataloging-in Publication Data
Names: Young, Denise, 1955– author.
Title: When we are seen : how to come into your power—
and empower others along the way / Denise Young.
Description: First edition. | New York : Crown, [2024]
Identifiers: LCCN 2024000618 (print) |
LCCN 2024000619 (ebook) |
ISBN 9780593239292 (hardcover) |
ISBN 9780593239308 (ebook)
Subjects: LCSH: African American women executives—
United States—Biography. | Leadership—United States—
Biography. | Women—Employment—United States. |
Emotional intelligence—United States.
Classification: LCC HD6054.4.U6 Y68 2024 (print) |
LCC HD6054.4.U6 (ebook) |
DDC 338.7/61004092 [B]—dc23/eng/20240213
LC record available at https://lccn.loc.gov/2024000618
LC ebook record available at https://lccn.loc.gov
/2024000619

Hardcover ISBN 978-0-593-23929-2
Ebook ISBN 978-0-593-23930-8

Printed in the United States of America on acid-free paper

Editor: Libby Burton
Editorial assistant: Cierra Hinckson
Production editor: Sohayla Farman
Production manager: Dustin Amick
Copy editor: Kristi Hein
Proofreader: Sasha Tropp
Publicist: Mary Moates

9 8 7 6 5 4 3 2 1

First Edition

Book design by Betty Lew

Jacket design by Anna Kochman

To Leon and Margaret,
my first seers

"My soul looks back and wonders . . .
how I got over."

—CLARA WARD

Contents

Contents

On Being Seen

The night of the opening of the Apple Store on Fifth Avenue in New York, I felt seen. It was May 19, 2006, and at 6 p.m. we opened the doors and greeted several hundred people who had been waiting in line since the night before. It was our second New York Apple Store and the first 24-hour Apple Store in the world, so everything about the opening had to go above and beyond all that had come before.

Steve Jobs hired Bohlin Cywinski Jackson—the architecture firm that designed many of the Apple Stores, as well as the Seattle home of Bill Gates—to create something magnificent that could entice customers to visit what was essentially a basement space on Fifth Avenue. The result was a cube-shaped design wonder that housed an underground retail store accessible via a glass elevator and transparent spiral staircase.

It wasn't just the design that made headlines, but the vision to keep it open 24/7. The Stores leadership team was sitting around the table in Ron Johnson's glass office when we first discussed the viability of a 24-hour store in New York. Ron had previously transformed Target and, alongside Steve Jobs, had envisioned the Stores from inception. (Yes, Store is capitalized, because these weren't just any retail technology stores. These were *the* Apple Stores and, as we saw it then, an entirely new technology experience.) I was the head of HR and talent, responsible for the hiring and training of people and the culture within the Stores, an environment that proved ultimately transformative in the retail industry and beyond. I was, additionally, an active participant in the leadership decisions made for the Stores for more than a decade. I sat in countless meetings, debates, and discussions just like that one, where we obsessed over details small and large, such as the viability of an all-hours Store. Was the idea brilliant or completely inane?

We hashed out the concept, raising varying points of view, until I saw at least one path to the decision that I didn't recall anyone else raising. New York has a world-class arts community, from theaters to arenas, clubs, and performing arts centers; every performer, worker, craftsperson, artist, technician, and vendor who works nontraditional hours and owns or wants to own an Apple product would likely become a customer of this Store, readily frequenting it at 2:00, 3:00, or 5:00 a.m.

I believed this because I had been familiar with this world since I was a child. My Brooklyn-born mother had made sure I was well acquainted with the art and culture of NYC. And the lives of my New York extended family, comprising nightshift nurses, small business owners, researchers, photographers, and service workers, did not lend themselves to white collar conventionality. It was the recollection of the lives and journeys of my New York family, my Louisiana family, and my Colorado upbringing that informed the perspectives I'd share in that meeting and many others. In that conversation, my life experiences helped shape what would become a historic place not only for New York City, but also for the world. And of course, there was the fact that I was also the only Black woman executive in those rooms, contributing to the Apple Store vision and thought process—one that would make business history and a dent in culture as we knew it.

We believed that the city that doesn't sleep needed an Apple Store that didn't sleep, seeing and serving the people whose job it was to inspire, uphold, and serve the spirit of the city and the world. We also had the opportunity to serve another dimension of New York: the round-the-clock service population, those we have since deemed "essential," the human infrastructure of the city. We could enable them by attending to their growing and aspiring tech needs at times they could better manage—after all, an iPod Shuffle or an iPod Nano with a thousand tunes in one's pocket could be great company on a night shift, and for the pros, the switch to Intel processors for infrastructural IT could see its way to new enterprise activity.

The 24-hour store experience was envisioned as a people-first proposition, and this way of seeing the Apple Store Fifth Avenue experience would become part of Apple lore. In the "always open" vision we held for it, profit potential might not have made sense, but the opportunity to serve people certainly did.

The night we opened, there were many celebrities in attendance, along with the thousands of people who lined up to be first to see and experience the Store. The PR team briefed us on who we should expect: Mos Def, Harry Connick Jr., Spike Lee, and Dave Chappelle, among many others. Opening night would kick off our first 24-hour cycle, so Ron and I took the 11 p.m. shift to greet people at the top of the glass spiral staircase of the cube, as we nicknamed it. Soon, Mos Def and Dave Chappelle walked in and were guided toward us. Ron, in his always exuberant way, introduced himself and me. "Hi, I'm Ron Johnson. Welcome to our Fifth Avenue Apple Store. And meet Denise; she is our head of people for all the Apple Stores around the world."

Dave Chappelle looked at me—obviously Black, female, and introduced as an important sounding Apple executive—and with a wry smile and a direct gaze he said, "Ah, sister, head of everything . . . how's that going?" I laughed, nodded knowingly back, and said, "It's going fine. It has its moments."

"I bet," he said, his smile now signaling curiosity.

He knew what I was saying. And I knew what he was saying with that famous grin. Only a year earlier, Chappelle had walked away from his highly rated television show, leaving a situation where he felt he was losing himself, his voice, his sense of integrity. Perhaps he saw me, that night, with a little more sensitivity.

For me, it was a moment of unique recognition—not just any recognition and not just from anyone—and it felt important. Despite the influence I might have had at Apple, and my central role in leading the Stores, here was a public figure, a celebrity from my own community, someone I had never met, acknowledging the importance of my presence there, offering a deep understanding of what it took for me to get there. As we say, it hit . . . different.

We chatted a bit about the design of the Store, then everyone moved on. But that moment of being truly seen has stayed with me. Chappelle had the intuitive sense to recognize that life might've been a bit challenging and certainly interesting for this Black woman who stood before him atop a famous glass staircase, with a big job title at a world-renowned technology corporation. Few people witnessing the exchange would have recognized the significance of what was being said in those brief moments. But Chappelle did. I did. And for me, his response said much more. It said, "I understand what it means to see you here in this space, in this role. I get it. I see you, sis."

What does it mean to "see" someone? "I see you" is a common phrase in my Black community. I love those three words, how they're used, and how they make me smile every time I hear them. "I see you" can translate to "I applaud you; I recognize the truth, beauty, and realness of what you are doing." The phrase says, I see what you have done, I see the value of *you*. It affirms, it connects; it validates and uplifts. One little phrase does and says so much, and even when this phrase is used in a social media context, where no one really knows anyone, it holds power.

At my workplace, as the first Black female senior executive at Apple, surrounded by peers who did not share my lived experience or background, I did not expect that same kind of awareness. As I was the only Black woman in so many rooms, my colleagues generally looked at it as an accolade that I succeeded where others had not. They did not register the fact that there were few "others" like me, although there were many like them. They were cognizant of the circumstances of their own paths to achievement but held little awareness of the added complexities of mine.

I rarely felt seen at work the way I did in other aspects of my life. This is common for women of color in technology, and in business in general. We talk about this, we build communities and networks to address it, we condition ourselves to it and knowingly accept positions understanding the baggage that comes along with it: that constantly being "othered" is exhausting and exasperating.

Over the course of my career, I learned to call on the resilience and determination of my upbringing to make my way in a world where I was frequently ignored, overlooked, unseen. It was never easy to navigate. But I had long ago determined it was what I had to do to work in this world, to earn money, resources, and means for my family and community. It was what I was taught to do in my era, it is what was modeled for me for generations and what I emulated. It was what we believed was expected by our ancestors, who held high standards and hopes for our achievement, based on their immense and often unfathomable sacrifices.

Along the way, though, something fascinating happened. Over time, I learned to lean *into* the fullness of my identity. Leaning *into* was different from Sheryl Sandberg's "lean in" philosophy, often defined as a "give it your all" kind of action. For me, leaning *into* meant building a progressive level of comfort with who I was and what I brought with me. Leaning *into* meant absorbing, sitting with, embodying.

The word "into" as I am using it indicates a result, a change of state, a destination. It means looking back in our lives and revisiting the things, places, and ideas that make us feel most alive, most connected, and most inspired, and bringing those experiences forward, as if they were a special talisman to wear each day. It means applying life lessons in the same way we would business lessons learned on the job. Leaning *into* means losing the fear that if you do not see yourself reflected in the world—if you are a "first" or an "only"—the value of your experiences are worth more, not less, despite all the indicators that seem to tell us otherwise. And the more I leaned *into,* the more impact I noticed I was making and could make.

Over the course of my career, I felt deeply the amount of "othering" that came my way, but like many, I built muscles in spite and, actually, because of it. In a phrase, the more of me I became, the more me I was *able* to be. In time, I simply began to rely less upon others to see me, and to *see* myself and appreciate what I saw.

And who was I? This is a question we all must ask ourselves, to stay in touch with our authenticity and with the parts of us that can evolve and fuel our thriving. Who am I, what do I believe, and why? What parts of myself do I lead with? What needs to be seen and known? And what is important enough to hold within, protected from the casually uncaring or the culturally unaware? If I were starting a career now, I would ask these questions of myself and of a few trusted others every couple of years. The answers for me were clear enough, but I often was puzzled as to how it all applied to my work, when the profile I chased for years often named other attributes as the desired ones—the traits most of my male colleagues brought.

My career at Apple moved from recruiting for its Colorado manufacturing facility to become the first Black person—male or female—to sit in a C-level role at the company. I led teams that established more than four hundred Apple Stores around the world, as well as all talent and human resource functions for the company. I saw my mission as the human work fueling the success of the company's technology.

I have seen a world and traveled a life path that my colleagues did not know, and only few had read about in sanitized history classes. I sat side by side with people who could not fathom my childhood rooted in a Jim Crow South through my family's Louisiana roots. My colleagues had no contextual understanding of what I experienced and absorbed through lessons my parents shared at the dinner table throughout my upbringing. I was raised by people who remembered their own grandparents living one generation out of enslavement; parents who'd experienced Black Codes, navigated travel with a Green Book; grandparents who'd benefited from the Freedmen's Bureau and western migration; aunts and uncles who'd fought with their lives for voting rights, who'd sat-in, marched, and solemnly attended the funerals of assassinated leaders through a television encircled in a living room. For whom, from several states west, Medgar, Malcolm, and Martin were household names. These were the historical realities of my family's journey.

We all have our own unique backgrounds and we each make decisions about what we hold on to. I took every bit of mine with me and carried it into the front doors and conference rooms of Apple. It took time, but I learned to not diminish those elements of my life story, because in doing so, I was then diminished. And I realized that a diminished me was a less effective and unfulfilled version of me.

Each of our stories contains clues to who we are supposed to be when we are thriving. How we speak and walk, what makes us laugh, how we evaluate information is imprinted into us from our life experiences. Our brains store core memories, which influence our actions, decisions, thoughts, and biases. While one may never know what it's like to walk in the steps of another, listening to the stories and experiences that shaped them is always informative. It can shed light on why Leslie is reluctant to join a lunch excursion or why Paul is reticent in meeting rooms but perfectly personable everywhere else.

We are the sum of our experiences, and if we are seen, if people take the time to know us, we each readily offer valuable information on how and why we are who we are. In fact, as the question of my ascendance at Apple is frequently asked about, my response is as frequently—because seeing people is something I know how to do. For me, valuing how others exist in the world, and understanding what got them to where they are, greatly served my success as a leader, as a human being.

We live in a time when stress, burnout, under resourcing, undervaluing, and underappreciation are a baseline reality in many business settings. Folks I talk to have less time to pause to see, acknowledge, and process one another's humanity. We get no credit for seeing others, no amassing of likes, no public kudos, no gaming scores tracking, then rewarding us for the number of times we humanly engage.

It's amazing to me how for some people the act of *seeing* is simply existential, like drinking water, taking deep breaths, and thinking, whereas for others, adding the small and simple step of consciously registering the human condition of others is more difficult. But with intentionality and some practice, a minimal investment of time and energy to connect with others can yield disproportionately positive results.

During my career at Apple and beyond, I made a conscious professional choice to keep my focus human, even while immersed in world-changing technology and surrounded by colleagues and systems who did not always reward that focus. Apple would always be known for its products. I wanted it to be known also for its people.

How do we incorporate appreciating and acknowledging others into day-to-day life? Where do we fit this added complexity? How do we become advocates for the idea of seeing and knowing others? Why would we want to?

First, it takes recognizing the fact that our brain's neural circuitry is not fixed, and we have the capacity to train it to be more empathetic and compassionate. We can make a choice to use and engage the power to see others, even if there are studies to indicate that our natural tendency is toward egocentrism, and even if we are wired to be primarily concerned with ourselves. So yes, it takes effort to be more attentive to human interaction. Yet with some intentionality, we can allocate more space in our lives for others. It doesn't require as much from us as we might fear, and the benefits are mutual. Everyone thrives. And the facilitation of thriving is as critical to any other type of value creation that we learn about in business. Facilitation of thriving is personally powerful, and we can all become masterful at it.

These pages are filled with my experiences as a Black woman who rose to the highest levels of corporate leadership at one of the most famous companies in the world by creating the space, both personally and systemically, to see others. This book is for anyone looking to make real shifts in their places and spaces of work, as well as anyone seeking to have their voice heard and their humanity recognized. Most of all, this book is for anyone who has ever felt left out, unseen, ostracized; anyone who has been an only or a first. This book is for anyone interested in upending perpetual cycles of exclusion and in reclaiming our agency in the ongoing quest to thrive and belong.

Each of us is quirky and flawed, and brings our own history, habits, and beliefs to every situation. People come into the workplace with their distinct stories and life realities even before morning hellos. Each of us can be "othered" at any time. Cracking the code of human connection starts with seeing each other and believing that dismissing the presence or humanity of another human being is not an option—especially when there is so much at stake. In our work spaces—be they physical, virtual, temporary, permanent, remote, or in person—the time is now to rethink our immense power to motivate, inspire, and liberate each other. It's time to say, "I see you."

When We Are Seen

I See You

Who lives, who dies, who tells your story?

—LIN-MANUEL MIRANDA, *HAMILTON*

In December 2014, *Fortune* magazine published a feature about me titled "Apple's New Voice." When the article came out, I had been at the company for eighteen years—what felt like a professional lifetime—thirteen of them in leadership and senior executive roles. I led a global team that had by then placed over 425 Apple Stores across the world and had infused them with the talent and a culture that gave the world a new way of interacting with technology. I had achieved significant business credibility for my work, and in multiple countries, so how was I a "new voice"? I had been at it for nearly two decades—so why was I being recognized now? Indeed, I had ascended to a coveted corporate level and as such had become another "first," another historic "only."

So, although my ascension to be the first Black woman as a C-level executive at Apple was new, my impact had been long standing after years of achievements. As I was touted a "new voice," I wondered if anyone had taken note of the prior years, countries, and thousands I'd impacted. Who then, deems us *seen* or notable? Are we seen only by some, and what are the criteria? Are we heard only when others give credibility to our voices? I had questions.

My issue was not with the competent reporter who wrote the piece, but rather with the media's overall shallow interest in learning of someone's broader context, and therefore contributing to the very essence of erasure. The story's "Apple's new voice" slant felt narrow to me, given what I had already done, yet many people praised the recognition, and, in sort of a mystical way, the story both saw me yet overlooked me. Had someone in the process of publishing the article taken a thoughtful pause around what was being said about this "first" story, the entire piece might have served a different and more powerful result: the rare account of a Black woman ascending to the top at a renowned tech giant, her real accomplishments, her real challenges, her next steps.

If the *Fortune* team had simply asked me the question the way Chappelle did, "How's that going?" I might have asked them to write about the positive impact of my work on thousands of employees, and the many firsts they'd in turn achieved, and how seeing people has a powerful business and human outcome. It might have been of interest to know about the role a Black woman had played in creating a cultural blueprint that would change the consumer technology experience forever.

The experiences of women, and women of color, and especially Black women, taking a particular seat for the first time (often a seat she should have assumed long before) might have been insightful for white, male executives perpetually grappling with taking a "risk" to promote a woman. Had I been asked, or had I been allowed to use my actual voice, I could have shared insights that might have proven life affirming for others who looked like me.

But the point of the story was my "firstness," as a Black woman in the C-suite of the world's most admired tech company, and yes, this was newsworthy, but hardly my highest impact work. It was a corporate byline, not *my* byline. It was what others felt my story should be, the most favorable story for them, despite what I believed, or even what my represented community saw.

Had someone only asked, I would have shared the hard work that had gone into building a culture that served both people *and* product to astonishing results. Had that story been heard by more organizations, more leaders might have taken note. Instead, I was the eighteen-year veteran presented, inexplicably, as a "new voice." The result was a missed opportunity, for us and for them.

Growing up, I spent a lot of time around adults and I learned how to listen. I watched them intently and was rarely bored by them. I listened to their stories and their experiences. I especially enjoyed listening in social settings whenever there was alcohol served, as that meant two things. One, everyone spoke more freely, possibly more honestly and definitely with more humor. And two, I could manage sneaking a sip of my dad's coveted bourbon and never miss a beat of listening. The adults surrounding me were fascinating in what was said and unsaid. With body language, tone, and inflection, there were always master tellers of stories—stories (alongside a love of humor and the artful sipping of bourbon) that have stayed with me for a lifetime.

All this observed information certainly informed my professional journey. And although I likely could have made a great jury consultant, having strong observation and listening skills in a business where people *were* my business was absolutely a strength. Along the way, colleagues—mostly men—challenged me to be less like me, and more like them: *Don't observe, participate! Speak up! Speak out!* Sometimes I succumbed to the peer pressure, chiming in where, in my mind, there was no need to, debating for the sake of debate. To me, these behaviors wasted time, but they were the behaviors of the included. And if I wanted to be heard, seen, *included,* I sometimes had to mirror them.

My parents were raised under the adage that children should barely be seen and definitely not heard. This was very likely a cultural remnant of protection. Allowing children to speak very little lessened the chances of saying too much to those who meant harm to our community, a legacy my grandparents and theirs would have carried forward from post enslavement. In Black families of my era, children did not much participate in adult conversations, and frequently were made to leave a room. Within this cultural norm, children didn't hold opinions; children's thoughts didn't concern adults, and they certainly were not solicited. But my family allowed me to transcend this parenting adage, gently encouraging me to have a point of view. They did not shield me from adult talk, and if I was in the room, I wasn't viewed quite the way other children were. I was Leon and Margaret's smart little girl whom it was okay to speak frankly around. If other children were there, we were all sent off to play. But on my own, I was seen, often even included.

Listening in on adult conversations meant I learned of the day-to-day injustices abundant in life for a Black person in America only a few years beyond the securing of our civil rights. In a military town, I heard tales of the indignities endured in a military that was desegregated only a few years prior to schools and institutions. This way of life was all still new. And there were traumatic personal struggles from meager household incomes to philandering husbands, the consistently frustrating experiences of living while Black, promises never fulfilled, and loss, unfathomable losses.

Many of the Black members of our Colorado Springs community had migrated determinedly from rural South hometowns, many coming directly from Arkansas, Louisiana, Mississippi, or Oklahoma, very much like the migration stories Isabel Wilkerson told us of in *The Warmth of Other Suns*. Some we knew had inherited generational legacies of resources, like the Sapp and Bourgois families. Some proudly upheld a rich family heritage of achievement, like the beautiful Phoenix sisters, or the Morgan twins, Joseph and Justice, and Sy Smith, with their Colorado Hall of Fame sports legacies as amateur and semi-professional level baseball players. There were the scores of military families who left the South with a branch of the military, who came through Colorado on a tour of duty and decided it was a place to stay and try to build new lives . . . lives they hoped would be less touched by a newly desegregated South. All of them contributed to the fabric of the "foot-of-the-Rockies" community that no one had expected to find us thriving in.

We were sitting upon and surrounded by Native American landmarks, such as the Garden of the Gods and Seven Falls, and as a child in Colorado Springs I first learned of the existence of the American Black West, where Black cowboys were revered, even legendary. Their stories differed dramatically from the traditional white-centric western cowboy stories we were told by the local museums or Hollywood. I even recall seeing an old black-and-white photo of a half–Native American, half-Black woman who was said to tame and befriend black bears during her migration west. My parents knew her and attested to the claims. In town was a famed racially integrated jazz venue, aptly named the Cotton Club, owned by the legendary Fannie Mae Duncan, an entrepreneur and inductee into the Colorado Women's Hall of Fame; I went to school with her niece.

The local NAACP offices were housed in a building with a popular barbershop, beauty shop, and Black art gallery. Around the city there were large and small churches, a Black Elks Lodge, and two Black mortuaries, one officed with a real estate and tax accounting firm. In the late seventies a Black four-star general commanded NORAD, the North American Aerospace Defense Command, the unsuspecting facility built directly underneath Cheyenne Mountain, whose role was to protect the air sovereignty of the United States and Canada. The local Hispanic population was modest but solidly represented in the small business community, as entrepreneurs of restaurants, landscaping, roofing, and construction outfits. This all existed in a town known mainly for its natural beauty, for tourism and travelers, for three of the most prominent military institutions of the mid-twentieth century, and a slice of Americana largely uncategorized but historically very present. Unseen. But we were there.

Emanating from all of this was intriguing conversation, little-known history, and fascinating stories. I listened, I learned. I kept it all in a cherished place. From the humorous, I processed the art of wit, from the joke tellers, I heard the underlying pain. The angry voices were frequently betrayed by the tremor of their fears. From those scorned, I heard indignation, but sometimes also forgiveness. From those systemically wronged, I heard vigilance and knowing. From these stories I came to understand the enormity of what we bore as descendants of enslaved people. Family, friends, neighbors, visitors to my parents' home all confirmed what I already felt deeply: that there was much suffering in the world we'd inherited and had to now navigate. We had to show up every day, simply because it was our responsibility to all who had walked before us and to all who would step into the future. We stayed the course, because it was our responsibility to do so, our divine assignment. This was our beautiful, complicated, authentic existence.

And so I listened more than talked, a practice I still highly recommend. I observed more than ignored, and slowly but surely began to better understand who I was, what I had emerged from, and what I thought about it all.

As a young child I rarely "talked back" as it was called, a trait not much tolerated in our community; I was, however, a master eye roller and in constant jeopardy of being caught arching a brow directly at my mother when I thought I was out of her view. In all honesty, I had learned my eye-roll skills from her and perfected them with my girlfriends, particularly my best friend Claudia, an even better master of the skill than I was.

There was eye rolling and there was "the look"—the one you got from a parent or adult that you knew was a warning alarm—or the look a woman gave another about to spill a secret, or the look you got in church that said "you have three seconds before you see the back of my hand." In my experience, Black women have undeniably perfected the look. Our eyes curtain the light of our souls, and this powerful form of communication allows us to speak without words to anyone, about anything. The look is globally recognized. The look is feared.

I developed this communication strategy early, yet I could also execute a pullback split seconds later. If caught giving the look to an elder, one had only to quickly sneeze, cough, or otherwise contort, disguising and retracting it to feign clueless innocence. My mother clearly saw through this; however, she was likely impressed with the clear skills I displayed.

My mom did not much engage outside of church, shopping, and a few neighborhood gatherings. But sans cable television, she read the newspaper daily, avidly consumed the major network news (CBS, ABC, NBC) and held lengthy discussions on current events with her circle of friends, hot sauce seasoned with a dose of the "have you heard?" on local gossip. She had much to say about the state and condition of women and Black people and expressed herself assertively. She seemed, however, to have an innate sense of when to speak, when to quietly smile that smile that wasn't a smile, and when to administer the look. She, as did the women of her era, understood when a matter at hand was not one of submission, but of safety; knowing how and when to apply and take advantage of her demeanor as a woman of her era. She would often save her most fervent indignation over the day-to-day challenges of life for long soliloquies after dinner, when my dad and I were captive, doing kitchen cleanup.

My mother's life was not easy, growing up in Depression-era Bedford-Stuyvesant, Brooklyn, surrounded by a knives-out toughness and, as she told it, abusers of drugs, women, and life. She grew up a minister's daughter with five siblings, and as the oldest of the Dove sisters, she was a jewel to her family—pretty, fiery—yet she found herself trapped in the environs of the time. She learned to wear the demure minister's daughter's smile, responsible for the well-being of the family, just as her own mother sat dutifully in her role as a pastor's wife. All her siblings were kind, expressive, creative people, but with no real places or spaces to be seen or be heard. I observed my mother's indignation at being unseen, her strength, fear, and fragility. She could flash extreme anger, then shift into a still calm in the span of a moment, and my father and I were not spared these flashes of mercurial fury.

The same complexity existed in the women I observed while growing up in our church. In my head I called them the Smiling Sisters. They weren't actual sisters; "Sister" was their church title, and how everyone addressed them. Sister Harvey, Sister Atkinson, Sister Viola, Sister Betty. I watched them with pure fascination.

They were always manicured, groomed, and coiffed, often with glorious hats, worn in matching splendor with their suits and dresses. They wore makeup that was quick to rub off on you from a hug, likely because they made their own shades using a creative mix of Posner's and Revlon (lab-designed makeup for Black women to match the multiple and varied hues of our skin did not become available until the 1970s and was then sold at largely unaffordable department store prices). Cologne was a necessity and never spared, and a bright and popping orange or red lip was the fashion norm as well as what we loved to wear.

This was church, so legs were to be covered by nylon pantyhose that were always too light or artificially "tan" because no company yet made them true to our skin tones, we were nonexistent to these companies. The thick hosiery and the well-oiled sheen of their skin created a prism-like quality that defied the laws of light. It was a look recognized in any Black church in any community in America.

But the most important feature of the church sisters was their smiles. Glistening smiles that gleamed, beamed, and welcomed. Smiles that comforted, admonished, and warned. Smiles that said, "Yes baby, of course" as readily as "I would not if I were you." Smiles that accompanied "the look"; smiles that radiated warmth yet stood completely independent of what their eyes belied.

I observed how often these smiles did not match the somber regality of the bearers but told a different story. They smiled, but I all too often saw weariness, vexation, melancholy, impatience, anxiety, and disappointment. I saw dimensions of emotion I didn't understand at the time. I saw complexity, strength, power, and rich inner life. And I saw indignation so strong it demanded the shield of a smile, lest it escape and betray its bearer. In short, I *saw* Black women. Sometimes I would catch one of the Sisters gazing beyond the benches and stained glass into some faraway place, a place of calm, of peace. Watching them in those childhood years honed my ability to see others, and to ultimately see and recognize myself.

Whether I realized it then, I was affected by the deep inner lives these women opted not to project but also could not hide. Observing them taught me that many things can be true about a person all at once. This was true not only of the Smiling Sisters of my childhood church, but of the visitors to my childhood home, the women in my workplaces, or simply people protesting untenable life conditions. Humans can hold many dimensions of complexity—from those who for centuries fled one country for the safety of another, to the noble "essential" workers who served the world through an unprecedented pandemic. The top-of-mind utterances that people voice is never their entire story, and if we choose to be observant, we can see more, understand more, learn much. We can, through mere observation, have a better sense of how and when to offer grace, space, or time.

The Smiling Sisters of my childhood were the prototype for women I have worked with throughout my professional life. In years of observing women, especially Black women, I have watched us grapple with sexism, racism, motherhood penalties, microaggressions, and all sorts of identity dynamics as wives, mothers, leaders, engineers, workers, caregivers, and more. Often women carry this weight, quietly dealing with enormous challenges to our personhood. So many who I observed or worked with tried to become more comfortable in their own skin, yet struggled mightily under the immense burden of societal constraints. I observed this internal struggle throughout my career, and because I was in HR I saw it up close, firsthand. And just as I did with the church sisters, I knew the stories behind the veneers were deep and personal.

But frequently, behind the closed doors of my offices, the veil was lifted, and people got real about being people. My roles were both official and personal, and I was often told far too much. Over the years, people shared with me the things they faced, believed, did *not* believe, and feared. I served as the eyes that truly saw things. Too often it was too late; a dam had burst. Under the fluorescent light, I could see the exhaustion, the weariness of carrying a load too heavy for both their work and their psyche. I saw their disappointment in managers and leaders they'd expected more from—more empathy, more wisdom, more benefit of doubt.

From time to time, rising from probably thousands, a story will rise to a conscious and vivid memory. I recall Marcia, so gifted and enthusiastic about her work, and mystified by her stagnant status, without promotion for years though she out-worked and served longer and harder than anyone in her unit. She persevered because each year she was told a promotion was being considered, yet only vaguely offered criteria or a reason why it remained elusive. Every year she harbored hope that she'd reach the constantly moving goalpost. It was irre-sponsible and careless leadership. I watched her hold hope for years, then quietly give up, shrinking into a version of herself that simply just showed up day to day.

I remember the guilt carried by Anitra, a working mother of a special needs child, penalized for being both a parent and a talented product manager. The latter required sacrifice of the former for her to be deemed *successful*. The demand of con-stant travel, in-person meetings, and managing the expecta-tions of executives who had no idea of the gravity of her personal responsibilities weighed on her and caused chronic stress and anxiety. Although I urged her to share some insight on her personal responsibilities, she opted not to do so and believed doing so would present even more difficulty, more barriers of perception.

I recall Althea's story. She ultimately relocated to another state, but not before the treatment by her team robbed them of her talents. She had been newly promoted out of hourly status and into her first salaried work, yet her all-male peers continued to interact with her as an administrator, as their inventory processor, saddling her with ongoing data entry, ordering, scheduling, and refusing to acknowledge her new title while offering her no time or space to train or learn her new responsibilities. Their excuse? She was "so good" at her former job. She believed she had to leave to be seen as a newly promoted professional, and finally did.

With Sherron, I remember her exasperation. The only Black woman attorney in her group, she was extremely intelligent and equally reserved. Her ideas, her voice, were acknowledged only when a more vocal and blond colleague echoed them, or one of her male colleagues echoed her, as though she'd never uttered a word. She tried to explain that this was not even subtle, until it overwhelmed her and she left, leaving behind a talent void that few likely realized, and even less understood. In her quietly different demeanor, the people she showed up for every day simply did not see or hear her.

I recall the invalidation in the eyes of Rae Ann (not her real name). Her real name, Savithreyan, had a multisyllabic pronunciation apparently too challenging for others to attempt to get right. So, she'd become Rae Ann, a partial phonetic substitute and convenient nickname offered by a colleague. She had essentially been renamed by dismissive coworkers. Reverently named by her family, she once raised the issue very pointedly at a dinner meeting, even offering pronunciation help. Everyone laughed at their feebly disguised attempts to even try pronouncing it, absolving themselves of any obligation to be respectful, continuing to call her Rae Ann, with continued accompanying laughter; laughter that she interpreted as mockery, humiliation that steered her away and to a nonprofit where her name was spoken with respect and honor.

These and scores more stories stayed with me, repeats of them, variations of them. They exist yet today not only in tech but in any and every industry. By and large, workplace culture is far from understanding the value and ultimate necessity of human-centered culture, where people are seen and encouraged to thrive. But for those of us who do recognize the gap, the urgency of it, for those who understand the depth of human impact and the immeasurable losses, we can take immediate steps to create new patterns. We can insist upon inclusivity where it is within our own reach. We can insist, and we can model it for one another. And the most expedient path to an inclusive environment is through thoughtful observation, as I learned at age ten, watching the people who sat in the pews and benches of my childhood church.

Seeing humanity in each other is not as inconvenient or time consuming as traditional corporate culture wants to believe. Acknowledging humanity at scale, for an organization, is not going to cause revenue deficits, but it *can* be the impetus for greatly enhanced enterprise success, just as it did for the Apple Stores, and just as it does in transforming relationships one by one, every day.

Chapter 2

The Earliest of Seers

Praise the teacher
that brings true love to many,
your devotion
opens all life's treasures, yeah.

—EARTH, WIND & FIRE, "DEVOTION"

When I was growing up in Colorado Springs, Miss June was the owner of the Dance Academy on Platte Avenue, and she was every bit the fast-talking dance mom of today's reality TV—except for the fact that she would often sneak out to the fire escape to smoke a cigarette, thinking no one noticed. I always did notice, and my nose would crinkle upon her return, tracing the same cigarette smoke I clocked on many adults. At that time smoking was acceptable indoors, but Miss June seemed to have an image she wanted to uphold, so she tried to hide the habit. I knew at some level that smoking was not part of the persona she wanted us to see. So I made a note to never mention it, seeing her need to not lead with it.

Miss June was a force. I began attending her dance "academy" at the age of four, and for every lesson I could not hurry my parents along fast enough to get there, tap and ballet slippers in tow in a tiny pink suitcase. My Brooklynite mother never learned to drive, but she made sure my father was available to take me to those weekly dance classes with Miss June. I studied pre-ballet, modern jazz, and of course tap, which translated to a group of little girls forming a baby version of a chorus line before *A Chorus Line* existed. My mother believed deeply in what artistic exposure would do for me at a young age. So while other kids were becoming Brownies and Girl Scouts, playing house, or learning sports, standard family fare for me was all about music, dance, plays, films, and museums.

In Miss June's Dance Academy, I first observed a trend that would follow me for much of my life: There were no other Black or brown girls or boys in my classes. It was as if no one had told them about it, yet somehow *my* parents knew. What special information did they have that other parents didn't? I don't recall exactly how I felt about this at such a young age. I just remember noticing this ever-present fact.

Growing up in Colorado Springs, I was surrounded by a diverse collection of friends, but when I took to dance, I was indeed the only Black child in Miss June's studio, the sole little Black ballerina in a sizable sea of kids of all ages. This difference manifested in ways that would become familiar. To start, my young body did not look like the others. I was curvier; they were more angular. And beginning at the age of five, my butt formed a bunny ski slope and had proceeded to black diamond by the time I was ten. The other girls' were flatter, and flat was the ballet standard; to not have a bottom that interrupted the desired body lines. Mine definitely interrupted. And while dancing, my head angled upward proudly and naturally. I'd be lectured that my head was "too high" and it would "throw off" my spotting and turning equilibrium, a technique I was adept at.

Then there were my feet, which were longer than most others', so my point arch was deeper and therefore actually prettier by dance standards. I had great extension, but was more muscular, which allowed me to execute clean jetés and tidy pirouettes, but perhaps without the extension or elevation others had. It is not dissimilar from what we hear today when we listen to a sports announcer speak on the differences in the body motion dynamics of gymnasts like Gabby Douglas or Simone Biles or the lengthy stride of a sprinter. We are built differently from the traditionally dominant culture standard, and as entrenched as we have become in the performing arts or sports world, we are still not driving a shifting of standards.

But more than anything, I loved dance. So dance I did, week after week, year after year, diligently. And sometime in the eleventh and twelfth years of my young life, I became quite serious about it. By that time my performances were no longer recitals of candy cane chorus lines, but full-length performances to Gounod's *Faust* and Chopin's intermezzos, *en pointe*. Miss June had retired, and my parents had found another dance studio for me. My new instructors were a couple: an American and a European, Marjorie and Keith, who had both danced professionally all over the world. I was in awe of them and their skills.

Though I believed I was a good dancer, I still convinced myself to hold back, to not expect too much. I'm not sure if that came from my "onliness" or from the subtle messages that somehow conveyed to me that "only" meant "different" and "different" equated to "not as good." I was not blond or pink, lithe or angular.

In 1970s Colorado, I did not fit the profile for serious ballet study, and my fellow ballerinas barely made room for me at the barre at weekly lessons. Unlike my first tiny dance peers, these older, more intense pink-clad girls made note of my differences at every turn. They were curious about my skin, touching it and asking questions. They commented about my feet, my butt, and—holy of holies—my hair. In and out of class, they would stare at my hair, whether in some form of braided up-do or evenly smoothed into its best French twist. Each time I stepped into class, I felt the invisible rising wall, requiring me to mitigate or defend my differences.

At this young age, and as an early "only," I routinely experienced microaggressions. I had no idea then that this too would continue throughout my life. I was now exasperatingly familiar with the feeling of being subtly excluded, of probing that bordered on ridicule over things I couldn't control, or of simply being deemed invisible by these girls. I remember sometimes it all gave me a tummy ache, but I would always try to ignore it away, as I loved the art of dance so much. But I know now that the experience depleted my budding confidence and any sense of my belonging in that room with these girls.

There are those people with the gift of knowing how to open a door, to shine a light, and to see differences as enhancement. My new ballet instructors, Keith and Marjorie, did just that for me. One day, they announced an upcoming performance, for which we would learn and perform Prokofiev's *Cinderella*. I'd not heard of that version, but I remember hearing the music for the first time and thinking it was stunning. And the storyline was far more vivid than the traditional fairytale in its telling of the bullied little orphan girl.

When the day came to announce parts, I sat in anticipation of what background role I might be assigned. Let's see . . . there was a prince, some sisters, a plumpish godmother. I figured I might end up as a mouse, a pumpkin, or even a ball attendee and wear a big fancy dress. But then I heard "Denise, you are going to dance the Autumn Fairy role."

I sat there for several moments, and my name was called again, as the rest of the principal fairies—Winter, Summer, and Spring—were all announced. The Autumn Fairy had a solo role. And as it turned out, she was me.

The Autumn Fairy swirled in with the wind amid autumn-colored leaves and made a dramatic entrance and exit. It simply did not occur to me this role could be for me. Although I was neither chubby nor awkward, the typical reasons for a dance studio to not cast a student, I was different. Yet, there I was, cast in this role where the music and choreography were soulful and full of personality, and where the fairy had something to say, like me. I was seen!

Once I got over the shock, my goal was to embody this opportunity. I felt as if I was the first Black girl to ever dance a major part on any stage, and I wanted to do it well. At the time my only role model was me. It would be a while before I'd become aware of dance pioneers Judith Jamison, Maria Tallchief, or Carmen de Lavallade. To this day I love watching Misty Copeland, Calvin Royal III, and Michaela DePrince. Because of these experiences I support the Dance Theatre of Harlem, Alonzo King LINES Ballet in San Francisco, and Cleo Parker Robinson Dance in Denver. Dance companies that develop Black dancers and choreographers, places where all possibilities are modeled for today's young ballerinas. But only a few decades earlier, the dance world was as white as the tips of the Rockies.

The life lenses of a unique pair of instructors who did not follow the norms of the era changed everything for me. They changed things for the audience that witnessed me, shaking up the unconscious messaging that only the little white girls in pink tights could be featured dancers. That moment shifted something inside of me as well, beginning to prime me for a lifetime of being a first or only; never having a manual on "first-hood," praying for others to join me in the halls of "first-dom," and always hoping that my presence was making it easier and better for someone coming along later.

The night of the performance, Keith and Marjorie smiled as they watched me dance. My parents beamed from their seats, perhaps even a bit surprised at this star turn. They'd sat at the kitchen counter with me while I decorated my hairpiece with sequins. They helped me dye my tights, steeping them repeatedly in a strong brew of Lipton's tea. We meticulously colored my toe shoes to match my skin tone—a chore Misty Copeland is yet today burdened with as she posted herself sponging her shoes with skin-matched pancake makeup. In 2023! I know that watching me on that stage was a moment for my family, affirming their efforts to teach and prepare me to do exactly what I was doing. Go first, work hard, be okay, be me.

In my few moments of whirling onto the stage of the Colorado Springs Fine Arts Center, I was seen. Up until that point, it had been messaged to me that my traits, hue, and body composition meant I should be happy with a background place on stage, but surely not a primary place. But honest teachers of the craft said no, and in an instant, interrupted that messaging. And for that night, and many thereafter, I held my long feet, curvy legs, and round butt more unapologetically—and everyone had to recognize.

I never got the opportunity to thank Keith and Marjorie

later in life, as an adult. And I often wondered how their experience as professional dancers informed what they did as instructors. I knew they would have a powerful impact in the dance world. In choosing whoever they believed to be the best dancer for the role, going against existing practices, they had enhanced their overall program as well as altered the self-perception of a young Black girl, and I hoped they'd done so for many more of their students. We can all do this in some corner of our lives—expand how we look at "cultural fit" to instead look to who and what would be "culturally enhancing."

We can live with integrity and authenticity, and there will be those who will see us, and those who will not, and always, those who refuse to see. That's the power of the seer: They make the decision to pause, look someone in the eyes, and unleash the force of human connection.

We can each likely recall a moment when a connective experience moved us, created a lasting memory, saved us from a crushing emotional fall or even shifted our life direction. The neuroscience behind human acknowledgment confirms that a physiological reaction takes place when we feel seen or acknowledged. The landmark Berkman and Syme study in 1979 highlighted the pure health and longevity benefits that accompany human connection.

For many, it was an attentive teacher, coach, family member, school nurse, or friend who made this happen. For fewer, it was a boss who made it clear that we mattered; who saw and heard us, dismissing the standard workplace dynamics, surprising and delighting the human being within. We are less likely to experience this type of connection in a workplace, and more likely to have "seen" experiences earlier in life. But we need these moments throughout our lives.

I'd argue that most of us have had an experience of being seen by someone in our lives in a way that altered how we thought of ourselves at the time. For you, was it so long ago? Does a particular moment or relationship still stand out for you? Why? Do you recall what you were seen for? Was it just for being you? Something you did well? Why did it matter? And is it important to remember it *now*?

My parents, Leon and Margaret Young, were my first and most important "seers," encouraging me to listen, learn, connect, and develop my voice in the world. They didn't always use these words, but they modeled it. What I simply considered to be their way of being and approaching parenting, I later realized was a deliberate and, frankly, courageous strategy in molding me and my belief system.

Another early seer was Ms. Zarle Sims, my high school literature teacher. She was exactly five feet tall, with a huge glistening afro. She introduced me and much of the tenth grade at Palmer High School to the Harlem Renaissance. She obtained special permission to teach this content, recognizing the need for Black students to hear these important literary voices as we moved through the tumultuous post—civil rights years, a questionable war and ongoing disappointment with a world where freedom fighting was ever present and ever perilous. Thanks to her, the epic writers of an important arc of time—Countee Cullen, Richard Wright, James Baldwin, Sonia Sanchez, bell hooks, Zora Neale Hurston, and many more—became a part of my literary lexicon alongside the requisite Twain and Shakespeare. It gave us life. Ms. Sims made sure we were conscious and "woke" ages before the word we'd always used to describe informed awareness was hijacked and weaponized.

Musical influences like my church choir director helped me to hear my own musical voice, the actual soul of it. Every stage I stepped onto throughout my career was built on the notes they'd first helped me to sing. And then bosses like J. James Brown and Dan Walker saw and encouraged my potential as a leader and made a point to tell me what they saw in me. Even Steve Jobs, all too often noted for diminishing spirits, offered approval at key moments after seeing our efforts manifested in an impressive Apple Store team and wanting me to know he saw what I was doing. And it started with two ballet teachers who resisted norms by casting me, a little Black ballerina, in a "first" role that would spotlight my truth as a young dancer, and ultimately as a leader in life.

I can look back and see how my life took shape—and see who contributed to that process. And when I look back, it becomes stunningly clear that when I was seen in both small or momentous ways, my personal GPS system was being programmed; my being was solidifying. Now dots connect for me when I look back and revisit these moments when others took the time to truly see me. And those connections inform my thinking to this day.

Because of this, I intentionally strive to *see* others, knowing that doing so holds a very universally human kind of power, a source we all can tap into. Our desire to be seen, to be valued and to belong, is existential. Seeing and valuing sows thriving. It's my hope this book will teach you how to harness that power for yourself. As we move through life, the resultant impact we have on countless others will be vast and immeasurable.

Chapter 3

The Places Where Seeing Lives

Suddenly my world's gone
and changed its fate,
but I still know where I'm going.

—CHARLIE SMALLS, "HOME,"
THE WIZ

On a gray Saturday when I was around eight, my mother took me on our monthly shopping outing. I'd learned early (and very likely from my Depression-era parents and grandparents) the art of stashing money away. Not only did I rarely spend the whole of my allowance, but I belonged to the school savings club, where a local bank collected a modest weekly amount from the kids in my class, and we'd each end up with up to $25 at the end of the semester! I had a little red suede bag I stuffed with dimes, nickels, and quarters, and double hid it in a closet. As a result, I always had a decent little stash ready to fund these shopping trips. I got to pick one store we would like to go to as a reward for accompanying my mother on her routine stops at the grocery store, dime store, and (for me the most boring of all) the massive furniture store my parents loved to frequent.

My passion at the time was buying 45 rpm records and

comic books. My favorite 45s were anything Motown, which I could buy for less than a dollar, and I could take home a couple of my favorite Archie or Lois Lane comic books for fifty cents. That left me with a bit of change to spare to look for the more rare comics featuring the fabulous redheaded reporter Brenda Starr. It was beyond fun, and was, along with my love of reading dictionaries and encyclopedias just because, well along into nerd-dom.

Mom and I had visited the appliance and electronics store for my beloved 45 rpm records that day, and I was clutching my bagged purchase, peeking into it over and over, when I realized I didn't see her anywhere. I looked around, walked the aisles, searched, and called out, but no Mom.

This is the moment in TV music scores where a crescendo of threatening music swells to alert you that a kid is in trouble. Not so much for me. I was concerned, but not afraid. The salesmen didn't seem to notice the well-dressed little Black girl wandering their store looking for something she couldn't find. But I was prepared for this moment, and I knew what to do, and how to get home one way or another. I had given my mom time to find me, so I thought, *something must have happened . . . maybe she couldn't find me and just decided to go home without me.*

I calmly wandered outside and a few more feet down to the corner where parked taxicabs sat. Knocking on a car door, I announced to the driver that I was lost, or rather, that my mother was lost, and that I needed him to take me home.

"I have taxicab money, and if I don't have enough, I have more money at home," I told him.

He asked me for my address, which I stated without hesitation, and he opened the door for me and took me to my house, about ten minutes away. I had been given the "strangers" lectures; however, I believed this taxi driver's job was to get me safely home to my parents. And he did.

I arrived home to a frantic father, who told me Mom was still at the store, upset and searching for me, and the police had been contacted. That's when it dawned on me: I would have to figure out how to explain to my mom why I'd left without her. I wasn't panicking, but she was.

Dad thanked the taxi driver, who told him, "You'll never have to worry about that one, she knows exactly what she wants." In those few moments, the driver "saw" a kid who was lost yet surefooted, rendering him comfortable enough to bend the rules to get her to where she needed to be.

My life has been a long series of "seeing" encounters like that one. At eight, I was grounded in my community, my family, and a sense of belonging. I knew what I wanted and where I was going. I wish that sensibility had lasted longer.

When I was deciding where to go to college, I contemplated Colorado College, Juilliard, and a few other East Coast options. My father's only brother, my uncle Frank, graduate of Dillard University, Alpha Phi Alpha, college roommate of civil rights activist Andrew Young, and a school principal in Monroe, Louisiana, sat me down for a conversation.

"Little girl," he said, "you need to go to a school where you will be educated on more than academics, where you will learn how to survive and thrive, and where you will make friends that will stay with you for the rest of your life."

He didn't have to spell it out; I knew what he was talking

about. He thought I should go to an HBCU (historically Black college and university). He specifically referenced Dillard University in New Orleans, where he'd attended undergrad, or Grambling State University, a small campus in Northern Louisiana just miles from my father's birthplace, where my aunts still taught. My uncle knew from experience that these were places I would never feel like the token Black student and that my smarts would be noticed and amplified.

The majority of historically Black colleges and universities were founded in the late nineteenth century, after the Emancipation Proclamation, to create higher-education experiences for newly freed Black citizens. They were built for Black students who were unwelcome at or excluded from attending existing universities, even if new postwar laws said otherwise. The early HBCUs were spread across the South and Southeast, with a sprinkling in the West. Morehouse College and Howard University became more prominently known, but all these schools became meccas of history and belonging for Black students who otherwise had no pathway to an education. As W. E. B. Du Bois wrote in *The Souls of Black Folk:* "in a single generation they put thirty thousand black teachers in the South, they wiped out the illiteracy of the majority of black people of the land."

Today, 107 HBCUs produce 20 percent of all Black graduates and 25 percent of Black graduates in STEM (science, technology, engineering, and mathematics) related fields. A McKinsey Global Institute Study states that graduates of HBCUs are 51 percent more likely to move into a higher-income quintile than graduates of non-HBCUs, making a case that our nation's HBCUs still positively impact Black economic mobility.

I knew little of these stats. I simply wanted to learn and thrive just as my uncle had described to me. I did want to make friendships that would stay with me for life. I yearned for music, experiences, food, and culture, to inform and enrich me on the many days of my journey when I would need it most. In the end, it was an easy decision.

When I decided to attend Grambling State University, my dad's extended family was ecstatic. My Uncle Frank's hunch had been brilliant, and I tell him so to this day. For the entirety of my life, he saw me, and, I learned much later, he'd partnered with my dad in quietly guiding me through some of my life's greatest challenges. And so I packed my bags for Louisiana.

The adjustment from Colorado to the Deep South was greater than I anticipated, even with family nearby. Despite Grambling being an all-Black college and town, it was a change to live in a rural southern town. But eventually, I got used to the humidity, super-sized bugs, rich food, and slower pace of Ouachita Parish, Louisiana.

Grambling, named after the town where it was situated, was its own new world. The school was formed at the turn of the century, to educate more teachers for the growing numbers of farms and farmers populating the rural South post emancipation. The French dominance of the state of Louisiana gave the schools and students a kind of flavor and flair not found at HBCUs outside of the state.

There were very old (historic, they told us) dormitories with nonworking elevators, combined with high-rise dorms recently built but with inadequate maintenance staff, as students themselves did what they could to repair screens, faucet handles, or furniture. But none of this mattered much in the face of hair-braiding marathons in the dorm rooms and lobbies, bid whist parties, and step and stomp rehearsals. Music played constantly: live, recorded, soulful, swagger-filled, and soundtracking our daily lives. I was enamored, as were most, with Grambling's dazzling "Marching Tiger" band and Divine Nine fraternity and sorority culture. I encountered young Black students who were focused, vocal, and proud, not only for their emerging achievements but also for their mere ability to survive. In retrospect, I was among future leaders, politicians, judges, playwrights, award-winning athletes, musicians, artists, and scientists. My uncle was right. Growing up in Colorado, I had not experienced this intense kind of energy even within my own community, and I was ready to embrace its power.

And as a young Black woman, I felt a sense of proud admiration from young Black men on campus. They called us "queens," and there was a reverence that accompanied even the typical college shenanigans. It was the first time I felt seen for my beauty as a Black woman, the first time I felt I possessed a tribal kind of beauty versus one designated by magazines or television. It was quite glorious.

Most of all, I loved Grambling's campus slogan—"Where Everybody Is Somebody"—which might have felt trite to the casual observer but was a resounding truth for students who came to campus from all over, from small rural towns to big cities. It rang true for the ROTC officer or chess master who was as respected as the basketball forward. It was like what Charles Blow, who would go on to write bestselling books like *The Devil You Know,* said of his time at Grambling: "During my schooling, all of my spaces were safe. Almost every classroom I ever walked into, a Black person was the smartest person in that room, so as an adult I continued to believe that into every room I walked I could be the smartest person there—it produced in me an overwhelming confidence, and also an ease of spirit."

I had been on the campus of Grambling for a semester when I walked into a session of Miss Lee Grant's literature course, a freshman requirement. She was a well-known professor and was feared by students for her "not today and not here" style, and well known for her infamous black walking stick. After a week or so, she announced the date of the first examination and how it would be graded. She looked at me and flatly stated she would be using a higher grading curve with me.

I did not have the courage to question Miss Lee Grant, but perplexed, "the look" did emerge, as much as I tried to manage it. She stated she would be grading me on a higher curve than the rest of the class because it was "too easy" for me. She didn't want me wasting my time at "lesser efforts," she said, with a hint of sarcasm and likely a response to my look.

At the time, I simply accepted this as the way of Miss Lee Grant. Looking back, I would realize this was the first time I saw that equity did not mean treating everyone equally; that sometimes you had to treat people *differently* if you hoped to set them up for the greatest success. Miss Lee Grant saw me and dealt with me accordingly.

At Grambling, I went on to take every class that caught my attention: molecular biology, ethics, public relations. This made it difficult for me to settle on a major, because so many things interested me. Eventually, and after the longest possible stall, I declared myself a writing and media major. Learning to tell a story that might move and influence was the educational foundation I believed I could launch from. I bolstered my core studies with music, dance, and science classes. I was delighted to be welcomed by Grambling's dance troupe, Orchesis, a jewel of an organization led with rigor and discipline by dancer Dr. Catherine Jones Williams, who'd studied under Katherine Dunham. The real deal, Dr. Williams recognized immediately my background in ballet training, and our troupe toured to perform at other college campuses. Known for a soulful and graceful dance style, we became the first women allowed to "dance front" Grambling's famed Marching Tigers band. We premiered this moment of HBCU history at the first New Orleans–based Bayou Classic.

But campus life wasn't all perfect. My first dormitory, Phyllis Wheatley Hall (every dorm was named after a historical African American figure), was clean and well maintained but also fraught with a theft ring I fell victim to. I also had a series of undesirable roommates until I was blessed with a string of great ones—some who became friends for life. The neglected classroom buildings or other facilities were not the fault of the school staff, who tried their level best to maintain them, but the result of years of disparate levels of funding that Black colleges received then—and to this day. Yet we thrived or learned to try to do so.

At Grambling, there were about four thousand students, all quite different. Hailing from as near as New Orleans or as far as Chicago, Los Angeles, or New York, some students came from well-off families, the children of dentists, doctors, and lawyers. Most did not. I was somewhere in the middle. Many endured more hardship than I could imagine to find their unique place on the storied campus. Married students separated from their spouses to attend classes, and single moms left babies with parents during the week, forfeiting college weekend frolicking to instead head home and attend to raising children and helping struggling families. A young woman and classmate of mine unknowingly in her third trimester of pregnancy gave birth in the community area of our dorm. Several students left campus abruptly for a lack of funds—their families initially thought they could pay but had competing survival priorities. Many students had never left their Louisiana hometowns. Despite these differences, we assembled at this small college to embark upon our idea of greatness together, and at Grambling, you weren't lesser because of how you'd arrived there.

In some ways these stories are unique to the HBCU experience. Some, like me, showed up via an airplane with a trunk packed with nice clothes. Others would be dropped off with belongings in paper sacks and pillowcases. There were students there only because their entire community had committed the resources for them to stand and represent as the first of their town to be college educated. The HBCU gets it; they know and they see. There are standard jokes about the long lines at the registrar's office at an HBCU because nearly everyone has an entry story, a glitch to admission, a hurdle to clear, and clear it they did.

HBCUs have always understood that most of their students had the potential for greatness. Yet so many needed something more, or something different to help them get there. Each student had to be individually seen, heard, and understood to best enhance their gifts. Not all would receive the same kind of support or teaching approaches. That's why Miss Lee Grant required me to score 4 percent higher on a test, while some students were allowed to retake exams when necessary. The faculty understood they needed to stay flexible in order to help all students achieve.

Was this fair? From an uninformed perspective, possibly not. But we were yet emerging from the economic and social devastation of four hundred years of enslavement, working still to survive and thrive in a society amidst those with varying degrees of privilege. How would we catch up? Creating an environment where everyone could thrive, no matter their back story, was the way forward.

That philosophy, if applied to corporate America, could be critical to the success of building diverse teams and assuring compelling outcomes. In his forty years of research on organizational behavior, Harvard scholar J. Richard Hackman found that successful collaboration (aka the best teams) couldn't be attributed to the personalities or individual styles of the team members; rather, teams needed "enabling conditions" to thrive. Specifically, he highlighted compelling direction, a strong structure, and a supportive context—meaning the environment in which people found themselves was linked to their potential.

Similarly, in 2012 Google set out to assess what factors led to great teamwork. Their research showed that the most successful teams shared behaviors like taking turns in conversations and showing empathy for others, which create an environment of psychological safety. Had either Professor Hackman or the researchers at Google observed an HBCU environment as a case study for creating team excellence, cultural competence, and true equity, they might have found a perfect model for what great supportive teamwork looks like. I am still amazed, given the statistical success of HBCU graduates (40 percent of all Black engineers, 40 percent of all Black U.S. Congress members, 50 percent of all Black lawyers, and 80 percent of all Black judges), that this simply has not been seriously studied.

A good friend of mine, a sales manager in a well-known tech company, recently shared that every conversation he'd had with coworkers on the topic of equity shifted quickly into a debate on reverse racism. The two concepts were deeply connected for people, and the difference between equity and equality remains profoundly misunderstood, even today.

In the minds of his coworkers, providing professional development or access to coding resources for a young Black systems engineer who needed more technical exposure was unfair to others. It was too hard to see this kind of help as optimizing talent potential, too hard to explain to other (white) colleagues who stood ready to point out any perception of unfairness. "How was this fair?" they would ask, ignoring the preceding years of unfairness to this young man, his family, his ancestors.

Similarly, according to this same group of coworkers, it was "fair" to pretend not to know the circumstances of a single mom of three kids on their team, all of whom had to be dressed, fed, and delivered to three different schools before 7:30 a.m. They required that she still make the 7:30 a.m. client download meeting in the interest of "getting a start on the day." Requests from her to shift the meeting by only thirty minutes were declined, as it was not "fair" to shift things for one person.

Small shifts and modifications can let people know they are seen and valued specifically for their unique circumstances. HBCUs have always understood this, but companies and leaders still do not. Or, perhaps the inevitability of backlash will always rear its head, setting us back, and limiting a better state for everyone. People are profoundly unique, so we must treat individuals differently to treat them fairly. Seeing and registering their differences, possibly accommodating aspects in differing ways, yet simultaneously believing in the talent and value people offer, is what HBCUs have historically done so well. Because HBCUs served student populations that had been so systemically disenfranchised, and consequently, so many students whose life experiences were so dramatically impacted by it, the schools have mastered the art of seeing.

Chapter 4

No Black Boss in Sight

I met a girl across the sea.
Her hair the gold that gold can be.
Are you a teacher of the heart?
Yes, but not for thee.

—LEONARD COHEN, "TEACHERS"

I waited long into adulthood for her: Tiana, the only black princess in 100 years of Disney's presence in our collective psyche. As an adult, I shamelessly took myself to the theater with no daughter or gaggle of girls I could claim to be accompanying. Tiana was a Louisiana girl, talented, hardworking and resourceful, until, under a spell of an envious spirit, she is transformed into a frog after kissing a prince who has also been turned into a frog. And, I was disappointed to learn, a frog she stays for much of the movie. Where was her star turn, her shining moment wearing a gown, her spot-lit vocal solo on the balcony of a castle? Instead, Tiana lived dutifully as a frog, taking a matter of fact approach to her challenging journey.

So, what did the first black Disney princess finally mean to me? That family teaches us what is most important, that we may live life unnoticed, that our gifts and talents prevail and always serve us, that sometimes we kiss life's assortment of frogs in order to break free of the spells cast our way. All those years of waiting for my own princess, and it turns out, I already knew her story. Sometimes we have to wait a very long time for someone who looks like us. And yet, we still figure it all out. I have had one Black boss in my entire professional career. One. That is a very long time to go without working for anyone who looks like you. I've had many professional people in my family—educators, scientists, nurses, and doctors—all important figures in the shaping of my life. But I did not work for them.

Think of the inverse of my experience: How many people do we all know who, over the entire course of their working lives, have had only bosses who look like them, think like them, and have had the same cultural touchpoints? For women, and for underrepresented groups in America, it is still not the norm to work for someone who looks like you—especially in STEM fields, where representation is still so dismal.

Members of the dominant culture rarely consider this idea. For them, it is the norm to always have worked for, been led by, taken direction from someone who looks like them, feels familiar to them, and shares life context with them. This is easily tested out anecdotally in two ways. First, when a brown or Black person is "placed" in charge of a dominant-culture group, especially a white one, everyone notices the race or ethnicity of the new manager, and discussion will ensue. Second, in industries or jobs with specialized professional training—physicians, technicians, financial officers, "chief" anything—there is still that two-second delay when a Black or brown person introduces themself as the doctor, chief, lead attorney, or most senior person in charge. So much so that the "Let me speak to the manager—I *am* the manager" scenario is a common sitcom plot. Its absurdity is funny, and its commonality is absurd. Entertainment, sports, and service work is still where people expect to see more Black and brown people, where there is an unspoken comfort level with seeing us.

Racism and racial bias lives and breathes without inhibition in the minds of millions, where it has become permissible to maintain a personal caste system. Have you not observed the quickly adjusted expressions of travelers boarding a plane when they glance into the cockpit and note the pilot is Black? I have. I have witnessed the brow lift on the face of a patient when a Black physician enters a hospital room. My relatives who are physicians have. And either I or many of my BIPOC colleagues have been *that* manager who steps out confidently at a customer's request, only to be stared at in disbelief.

I know well the disoriented look, the awkward smile of *How will we interact now that it is clear to me you are in an authoritative role?* Those moments that cue in our biases like a soap opera soundtrack. Ask any Black or brown person about that "moment of recognition" and we will tell you: "I've lived this moment throughout my life." And yet, had an African American person of power and authority walked into my place of work over the course of *my* life, I'd have experienced that same five-second delay—but registering instead a current of surprise and delight at the realization!

After graduating from Grambling, at first I considered staying in the South, maybe New Orleans, Houston, Atlanta. I loved the idea of writing, reporting, investigating in one of these cities, and I even met with a few news outlets, but in reality I was not sold on becoming a full-time resident of the South. College years in the Bible Belt South taught me a lot about mindsets and mores. The sense of southern traditions could be pleasant and inclusive, as much as they could be startling, disconcerting, polarizing, and othering. And as much as I loved being part of a campus where I was not an other, rarely a first, and hardly ever an only, I needed to breathe slightly cooler air to clear my head. So, like many college grads, I moved back home, because I knew enough people in Colorado to network myself into a job until I decided on my next move.

I was hired as a program officer for a nonprofit consortium that worked to make other nonprofit agencies—like the regional chapter of the Red Cross or the Women's Resource Agency—better structured, funded, and generally healthier. I was assigned to the fundraising arm of the organization and was, in short, miserable. Each day came with a set of reports for potential prospects, partnerships, and alliances I needed to call upon to fund the mission of member agencies, and I was to reach out to them cold for possible contributions. I had to ask for money. I barely would ask even my own family for money. It was hard for me both personally and professionally, and anyone could see this was the case.

My boss, a tall, thin, blond white woman, instinctively noted my lack of confidence in fundraising. Despite how much I detested it, I worked very hard at it. When I connected with a funder, I spent time talking and asking questions, trying to find a point in the conversation where a request of a cash or in-kind contribution felt more natural.

I hoped my boss would flash me at least a nod, an acknowledgment of my efforts, or perhaps offer me suggestions. Instead, she would call my name out specifically in staff meetings (and write it on a large whiteboard), drawing attention to all the funding I had *not* secured, reading my individual report out loud line by line with increasing emphasis. I was mortified. I tried meeting with her privately, but that took a worse turn.

She relished informing me that I was failing, missing goals, and just generally screwing up. I feared every week that I would be fired, not because I might not find another job, but because failure of this sort was foreign to me. Every evening, I'd stay up to study my projection sheets and plan for the next day, all in hopes of securing any amount of commitment. But nothing worked. I was profoundly uncomfortable asking people for money, and no one coached me on how to do it. I never even suspected that—as I learned much later—I had been given a "low likelihood" list to work with. A list of "dud leads."

This cycle continued for some time until one day I was pulled aside by J. James Brown, a tall slender, reserved Black man who worked as an executive program director at the agency. I think he had simply tired of watching me repeat the same humiliation loop with my exasperated boss, my low potential lists, and my look of defeat. He asked if I was interested in moving into his department. I remember gasping and almost hugging him—though I had little idea what his department even did.

As it turned out, it was a perfect match for me. He ran the organizational development side of the agency, which worked with organizations on their leadership team selection, finding and placing suitable board leaders, reviewing their mission and service offerings, and building authentic community relationships that were less transactional.

Voilà! I had unknowingly secured my first HR job. I loved the work and was good at it almost immediately, even with the learning curve. And I became J's shadow, perhaps to his chagrin. He was quite brilliant—well-educated, analytical, composed, and savvy. He operated with equal parts empathy and strategy. And aptly, given that we worked with nonprofit agencies doing hard and noble work, he was full of compassion. I wanted to learn all I could from him.

He knew this, and he pulled no punches behind the scenes, teaching me how to navigate boardrooms and combative meetings, listen to different types of people, ascertain who held the power to make decisions, and spot potential trouble. He taught me the importance of keeping confidences ("loose lips sink ships and lose jobs"). He told me, "You're going to find yourself in a room where you know things, but they cannot know that you know." I am pretty certain he told me this because I possessed "the look," and in these settings that infamous expression might inform key people we saw directly through their BS. I learned to model his composure.

Witnessing a Black man exert the level of influence he had, influence that resulted in a flow of needed social services across Colorado and beyond, and having him share this knowledge freely with me, was joyful. I held him in such high esteem. And as it turned out, we actually saw one another. I saw him as a quiet and effective force who didn't always recognize his own mastery. He drove results and wielded influence, was great at both managing and leading, was smart and astute, and was the key to the success of dozens of agencies, who in turn served and helped thousands of people. Yet someone with a grander title or large bank account would often take public credit for J's outcomes. My esteem for him only grew as I learned how incredibly valuable he was and how minimally acknowledged. Having a Black boss had taught me much more than I realized about the realities of being Black and professional in America.

left that job (and working for J) to work for Apple at its Colorado facility in 1996. When I told him the news, he teared up and said, "I knew from the beginning you were going to be great. I saw it. I am so glad to have had this time to work with you, and I learned so much watching you." From watching me? He had basically saved my livelihood and salvaged my self-esteem in the wake of someone intent on destroying it. Heading home that day, I was sad. At some level I feared I might never again have a boss as kind, brilliant, and who saw me through a shared cultural lens. I never experienced that again.

I have had some truly good managers and leaders in my life—ones who enriched my career and life in general or placed me in roles and situations where I learned much, fast. But never again did I experience the advantage of a boss who offered real, trusted, honest, insightful feedback, based in part on our cultural connection, but also on the safety and belonging we built with each other through that connection. People of like backgrounds or ethnicities don't always relate in this way, but when it happens it can be life changing. Representation truly does matter—for so many reasons.

Not that every boss since J. James did not see me, but most of my subsequent bosses responded best to the parts of me that were most like them (which was often not much). Instead of seeing the aspects of my personality that made me a unique asset, they tended to look for all the ways in which I was most like them, made them more comfortable, and conformed with expectations.

So in environments of my early career, the messages were clear that everything that made me, *me,* was of less value, and my chances of thriving were diminished. To the extent that we are tribal and seek out what is familiar, this practice makes sense. We are drawn to our tribes; it's who we want to sit with, laugh with, work with. If our tribe is absent from the table, we will struggle.

But even tribal communities learn there are desirable assets and alliances beyond the tribe. If we can only take a small step outside ourselves, see the less common, sit with the less familiar, much awaits us.

When you opt to create a vibrant work culture, you will encounter some tension and likely a language barrier with other functions, areas, and leaders. An often classically adversarial relationship has been with HR and Finance, or budget decision-makers. But great collaborating, seeing, compromising between the two can be pivotal to a thriving culture. Unsurprisingly, the core essential attributes of a chief people officer and a chief financial or administrative officer aren't the same. The people in these positions are wired differently, and the enterprise needs them focused on very different forces. But if the two were to see commonly the importance of thriving, many corporate cultures would follow that thought process.

Peter Oppenheimer served as Apple's CFO for years. When Steve Jobs passed away, my team and I began to work more closely with Peter, as he helped Tim Cook in his earliest days, weeks, and months as CEO to gather cross-company insight. What was most compelling to me about Peter was his ability to listen and be influenced if a good case was made. He demonstrated meaningful engagement at a high level. You felt heard. If one were to make a well-supported, balanced case that influenced a shift in his thinking, it might inform a critical company decision. I valued our interactions and felt respected.

That said, every division had assigned financial analysts to work through significant budget matters. I was kind of a dotted-line "boss" for the various analysts assigned to me over the years, who were almost always male, with almost always astonishingly low exposure to human issues and needs. As a representative of what was human-centered at Apple, I had to rely upon collaborating with an analyst to ensure approval for my projects, projects designed to support employees. From the hiring of significant talent, to their training and development, to offering tuition assistance, to cryopreservation (the process of freezing one's eggs to preserve for future utilization) and family-friendly benefits, I spent an inordinate amount of time with analysts with whom human investment was not their love language. Yet we needed each other's best efforts. Often, at a first meeting with a new analyst, I'd realize I was sighing as I knew how much work would be required of me and of my team to secure just the fundamentals of what I considered to be non-negotiable human investment.

One of my assigned finance partners, a fellow named Mike, habitually began tinkering with his Apple Watch whenever a conversation with me or my team became intense. A nervous tic perhaps, but it was frequent and noticeable. Or worse, he'd simply withdraw his presence altogether, as though he'd been given a teacher's pass to leave the classroom, to pay no further attention, with everyone else still in the room. He would sit and read texts, clearly indicating to me I was no longer a priority in his day.

Mike and I could not have been more opposite in style or philosophy, or even our goals. He was painfully analytical; I was inclined toward storytelling. He routinely wore pale blue oxford shirts and held himself tightly; I routinely wore colors and was expressive in style. Neither of us much enjoyed our time together, so it was easy to understand our lack of alignment.

One day Mike learned that I had family and roots in Louisiana. So did he, and in fact he traveled there more frequently than I did. He made a sincere attempt to find a way for us to share some small thing in common, asking questions about my town of origin, sharing stories about his.

I appreciated what he was at least attempting to do; I just wondered if he'd given any thought to the fact that his Louisiana history and mine were likely not a happily intertwined story. Our family's respective experiences might have made for an interesting launch into more insightful conversation. But I doubted we'd ever get that far into engaging around each other's back story. He simply needed a way to connect with me, and that was his way. I worked with what we had. I appreciated that he'd given thought to how to connect and made an effort. Our relationship might not have improved significantly, but it became less flat. We decided to try to see each other, however dimly.

Sometimes this is all we can hope for. Some critical relationships are simply not going to move into a thriving state, for many reasons. But when we try, when we make that effort, even the slightest improvement is worth the effort. And for me, just the effort made the uncomfortable less so.

In full days of work pressures and stressors, people have minimal capacity for learning about coworkers, even when it might improve relationships or entire functions. It's a lot; it's hard. We just do not have time to know more or to care. Caring requires energy. Caring requires that we feel. And few are willing to "feel" at work, especially among the dominant white and male cultures in tech and corporate spaces in America, those for whom "feeling" has still not been culturally endorsed. I recently came upon a passage in *Your Brain on Art*—a book my colleague Ivy Ross cowrote with Susan Magsamen—which rang deeply true to my experience. They quoted neuroscientist Jill Bolte Taylor: "Many of us believe ourselves to be thinking beings who feel, but we are actually feeling beings who think."

I knew well the truth of this statement. Almost daily my work in HR witnessed it. Yet in corporate settings, too often the idea of feeling or emotion was dismissed, diminished, or devalued in assessing or decision making. Eliminating it was the ideal state. And in my work, I have witnessed that lack of feeling generates a lack of connection, followed by minimal trust and even less respect. The absence of feeling in an organization sets to the side the opportunity for it to thrive.

What is the rationale for this resistance to feeling? It's simpler than it seems: We resist because it is hard, uncertain, and messy. Feelings are uncontrollable in a world we believe we must control at all times. There are always complexities to navigate when it comes to human beings, and in the spirit of avoiding that level of complexity, it has just been easier to overlook our humanness rather than accommodate it. It has been safer to pretend that the avoidance of humanity is acceptable.

We will declare it a matter of efficiency; who has the time in any given day to spend interacting with others? But is it really true that we don't have time or capacity? How can we encourage our minds to see, notice, inquire, and connect more naturally?

I have a dear friend who engages with every Uber driver, grocery store associate, events usher, and pretty much anyone she encounters. I would not call her an extrovert, nor does she engage in mindless chatter. She is genuinely curious about individuals and the how and why of their stories and lives. I have watched her do this for years, often exasperatingly so. But I also learned from watching her that she leaves a stream of lightness in her path. People respond to her in a myriad of ways, but she leaves behind a kinetic energy by feeling and caring. This practice also seems to fuel her.

As I've watched this friend, she's helped me to understand that people matter in the big moments as well as within the passing moments of each day, if not more so. Years ago, I watched the GM of a popular New York City hotel stand at the main doorway. I thought he was porter staff. He spent a few minutes at shift change times greeting everyone who came through his doors. It was a conscious decision, as he was an extremely busy guy. He, as well as my good friend who talks to nearly everyone, influenced me to do whatever I can each day to interrupt the patterns of "unseenness." It is simply a decision I made, she made, he made, and many in turn benefited. If we need to analyze that benefit, we already know it is an exhibition of emotional intelligence, that the seeing of others is a critical life skill that will impact the health, well-being, and thriving of those we encounter. Or, we may reason out that *seeing* people is a connection strategy we can apply to get work done, and be deemed more effective at doing so. With either parts of our brain, it bears out that seeing is profoundly inclusive, and that somehow not incorporating a way to do so is profoundly exclusive.

Logic then might say that actively, intentionally seeing others around us is a way of performing better and reclaiming our individual agency. A new way of reconnecting with power that in our reluctance to take time to feel, we have unknowingly relinquished. It is a critically important time to take this power back. In a nutshell, these are all lessons I learned from family, from Disney's Tiana, and from my one Black boss, whose quiet reserve, composure, and logic shifted my course in a big moment and many subsequent small ones.

Chapter 5

The Voices Make the Choir

Reverend Martin told us
what needed to be done.
And if he can preach it,
we can sing it,
help to make the new day come.

—MAVIS STAPLES, "MY OWN EYES"

When I was growing up, claiming membership to a Black church meant you belonged. You had a church home, a place of spiritual respite, a community of unconditional acceptance, a place where you were seen. My family's church, Trinity Missionary Baptist Church in Colorado Springs, minutes down the street from our house, was an extension of my life, my education, and the beginning of my study of human behavior. The Black church was that place that professed no solutions to the charged, searing issues of the times, but existed and thrived despite these challenges, even because of them. Enduring and strong, it offered comfort, community, and a viable path forward by virtue of its ability to see, hear, and extend the embrace of belonging. It was at once both solace and power, and a singular source of strength and survival for Black people in America.

As a young girl, I loved the feeling going to the church extended, consistently, every week. I loved the rituals, the rhythms of each service, the choirs, the musicians, even the scents and smells of woods, colognes, and the humidity of a baptismal pool always awaiting below the pews. I did not always remember or resonate with Sunday school lessons, but I loved the people who taught them, and their unconditional demeanor was comforting. I observed it all closely. Music made it even more compelling. I especially loved the connectivity of the songs, the voices, the rise and fall of the singing. The ways a song connected people, culture, and history with one lilted note or inflection. How a single recognized chord evoked the same feelings, thoughts, and shared history in any Black church in the country. I felt supremely comfortable leaning into the strains of music for cues to how life was supposed to look and feel. So to eventually find both my emotional and physical voice in the midst of this familiar and familial cultural experience made sense, yet it also left room to grow, even encouraging openness and acceptance, for all that would come my way.

Mr. John Bowen arrived at my family church when I was in middle school. This heralded new choir director from Chicago had studied with gospel music greats like Dr. Thomas Dorsey, who had penned songs for Reverend Dr. King during the height of the civil rights movement. Mr. Bowen showed up with a large leather-bound binder filled with his own compositions, and with a jaw-dropping list of credits and contributions he'd been making since he was a teenager from South Side Chi. He was known throughout Chicago's vast church community and was also an award-winning public-school music educator. Our little church was small, but our choirs were impressive and our choir members knowledgeable about the music. We were all giddy to meet our new leader. And

John did not disappoint. On any given Sunday, thanks to him on his Hammond organ, the church, the parking lot, bordering alleys, dogs, cats, and neighboring houses absolutely shook.

John Bowen was the real deal. He was quiet, yet exacting, and could direct from the organ bench with the smallest gestures. He seldom smiled, but when he did, it dimmed all other light in the room. He was one of the few men I knew who also possessed "the look," and used it judiciously in choir direction. I was mesmerized by him, and every rehearsal I would stand in my soprano 2 section and do my best to wail out the complex four-, six-, and sometimes eight-part harmonies he'd brought in.

After one rehearsal Mr. Bowen pulled me aside, and asked, "Ms. Denise, could you give me a few minutes please?" I eagerly yet tentatively made my way closer. He seemed oblivious to who might overhear as he asked, "I want to know . . . why are you shout-singing on these songs?" *Shout-singing,* I repeated to myself. Is that a thing I am doing? "You are not singing. You are working too hard, and I think you are trying to be heard, and that is not serving you. It is unnecessary. If you must belt these parts, you should not be singing them at all."

I stared at him, tears welling up, wondering why it had taken so long for someone to finally tell me that, actually, I could not sing. I was immediately angry at my parents for letting me go so long thinking I did have these skills, and I was deeply embarrassed.

He continued, as if I were not mortified enough.

"I am moving you to soprano 1, and I am going to give you some music to study. Do you read music?"

"Yes, I sight-read fairly well," I managed to mutter.

"I am sending you home with 'My Soul Is a Witness,' 'Over

My Head,' and an arrangement of mine for 'He's Got the Whole World in His Hands.' I want you to start listening to Leontyne Price and to Kathleen Battle. And let's have you throw in Tramaine Hawkins and also Deniece Williams for style and texture."

Then, quietly, he said, "You have a beautiful voice, but you are going to ruin it with all that screeching. That is not your voice. Sing in your voice, and don't stop singing until you believe your voice is as beautiful as I do, because you don't hear that yet."

Suffice it to say, my life again changed in that moment, in actuality and metaphorically as I processed the very idea of "shout-singing." His acknowledgment, in public no less, alongside a serious study assignment, was all the motivation I needed. He was so accomplished, so revered, for him to say I had a "beautiful voice" to me meant it was 100 percent gospel truth. Never mind that I did not yet know or believe that for myself. We often need others to see us first, to offer us external validation before we can see or receive it. I sometimes still don't, which makes that precious moment even more meaningful.

I went home, and threw myself into my assignment, embodying the assigned songs and emulating the sopranos I was to simply listen to. I read and listened to everything I could find with Leontyne Price and Kathleen Battle singing, learned several of their arias, and absorbed every spiritual Kathleen sang. At that age I was still missing the part where he said "Hear the beauty of your *own* voice." And that would take some time. In the meantime, Leontyne, Kathleen, and others were singing our history, my history, and they helped me find another dimension of my identity, my cultural strength. That essence would serve me years later in white spaces with no Black bosses, and where I was a first and an only. The essence that would prove to be my superpower not only for singing, but for existing. In due time I did discover the beauty of my voice. Without strain or force (or screeching), I learned that my voice could float, soar, hum, and be placed in ways I'd not realized possible—and still be heard. I learned it was not the force or volume of it that mattered, but its presence, clarity, and color.

Finding one's voice doesn't mean that you are perfectly eloquent, attuned, or profound at all times; to me, it means taking the time to understand what you're saying, why you're saying it, the impact it can have on others, and then finding the courage to use it. Very often, you find your voice when another person amplifies it, as master choral director John Bowen did for me at fifteen. Finding one's voice—one's superpower, that characteristic ignited in the times you are "seen" in life—it is worth the search. If you find it early in life, it is worth revisiting and remembering how it made you feel. If you find it later in life, that is absolutely okay. Use it.

We weren't a big sports event family. I was familiar with the legacy of Black baseball leagues and historically important players no longer in their glory, because they were heroes of my father's era. The most notable boxers and matches warranted family TV time, finding Dad and me mimicking sports announcer Howard Cosell, munching popcorn and peanut brittle, and drinking 7UP from the bottles. So while most everyone around us celebrated sports, my family celebrated art, and I was at the center of it.

My father's challenging upbringing and deep work ethic did not readily lend to what he saw as the luxury or leisure of sports. We rarely took family vacations, but instead routinely hosted others to visit. Through my mother's influence, we attended varied arts performances and, of course, my recitals. The exception to not vacationing was my mother's and my annual summer trip to check in on her mother, my grandmother in Brooklyn, and our relatives up the New England coast. There I'd gleefully spend the time in local libraries with my favorite cousin Jimmy and at the ballet or theater with my Aunt Sylvia. I'd visit New York landmarks with my Uncle Jim, the Pratt Institute Lab with my scientist uncle Ray, or the family photography studio on Atlantic Avenue in Brooklyn.

The art I was exposed to ranged from Gordon Parks and Romare Bearden to Lena Horne and Billie Holiday. My mother had her stories of seeing Billie and Lena at the Apollo; my photographer uncles carted me to exhibits in Brooklyn galleries. These experiences shaped me and informed my life views. My mother would tell me to appreciate the experience of art: "Don't just sit and look at it; take it in and it changes you. I want you to take all of this in and be different." Looking back, I now understand that "different" for her meant smarter, freer. It was something I believe she felt, and something she believed was important for me.

The first ever Broadway play I saw was *The Amen Corner* with Beah Richards. It was a James Baldwin work, produced by Maria Cole, Nat King Cole's wife. I was nine-ish and riveted by this very adult material, not completely grasping all of it, but knowing I was amidst greatness watching Whitman Mayo, Juanita Moore, and the great Ms. Richards.

My creative life started early through writing. On the pages of my lined Big Chief tablet you'd find scripts for imaginary characters, or songs to be sung at the top of my lungs from the basement laundry room. I started singing at a young age in church and school choirs, then studying dance as seriously as one could in a small town, later becoming a touring dancer in college. Ultimately I figured out how to integrate my business life with a performing life, singing on music festival stages, in cathedrals or symphony halls, between jetting to new cities finding and training the talent that would bring to life Apple products inside of Apple Stores across the world.

When I first met Daniel Haynes, I was still living in Colorado, working for the City of Denver and taking grad school classes in organizational development. And of course, as I always managed to do, finding time to seek out music and musicians, finding my tribe. Danny was a gifted pianist, and we had an immediate understanding of one another; very "cosmic," one of his favorite words.

Danny lived in a loft in downtown Denver with a collective of musicians who all performed their own compositions. Although they mastered multiple genres they played mostly jazz, and I sometimes sang with them. It was all very Monkish, if one could assume what that experience might have felt like. The loft's intimate audiences were eclectic and included everyone from other Denver-based artists and members of Earth, Wind & Fire, to local politicians, club owners looking for talent, and former Black Panther Bobby Seale and his brother John. It was a heady existence for a twenty-three-year-old, serious about music, life, and suddenly love as well.

I never tired of hearing him play piano, playing as he did the full breadth of the instrument with brilliant dynamics, complexity, yet a straightforwardness that had you hold the music with you long after hearing it. We talked incessantly, and he never seemed to tire of my endless desire to solve the world's problems. We were idyllic, yet still somewhat grounded given both our backgrounds. We moved into a small house together, and only after I discovered I was pregnant did I understand just how far out of my familiar life realm the relationship had taken me. The fact that a child had been created jolted our idealistic existence, challenging it with realities, but exciting us both with who and what this amazing child would become. Daniel had dropped out of college due to a lack of enough money to pay out of state tuition and to pursue a recording contract that didn't materialize at the level he was promised. His family was fragmented, and his upbringing included considerable hardships, including his mother's untimely death. I'd had a life journey that allowed me to bask in music to thrive, he'd grown up bathing in music simply to survive.

He saw me, however, in profound ways that transcended the romantic. He called out my love of writing and storytelling, and the fact that I loved being backstage as much as being onstage. He saw my pace of always being steps ahead of others and therefore annoying as hell and impatient with those slower to come into my vision of things. He recognized that I would give grace to anyone who asked it of me, deserving or not. He told me I would be successful in ways we only dreamed of.

In turn, I saw the nuances and competing forces within him. He wanted to be a competent session musician for the more reliable work and income, but his fingers constantly created something new as they touched each key. He could not sit still, not from boredom or restlessness, but from the mere velocity of creativity. Like me, he portrayed calm on the outside, but unlike me, he was conflicted and yearning to explore any and every possible turn in life. I saw this, and with all the love, care, and hope I held for us, knew neither of us was inclined to conventionality in a relationship. Yet it was an ethereal match.

By the time I introduced Daniel to my parents, my pregnancy was apparent, and so we faced the obvious questions:

"Are you going to get married?"

"Where will you live and raise our grandchild?"

"How will you do this as a working (or nonworking) musician? What will our daughter's life be like?"

The whole "getting married and having a family" thing had never been a priority goal for me. I had gone to college with and met amazing young men but remained largely uninterested in that traditional life trajectory. There was too much to do, to discover. I valued independence, expression, and experiences, and had started to think more about a career versus a "good job," and what that could be like. I loved the idea of love and what we had come to understand so far about it, but marriage seemed like something for other people, or maybe for me, much further into the future.

Daniel knew this about me and, in an attempt to be supportive, said to my church-going parents, "We don't really need to marry traditionally; we are divinely connected, and our spirits are united for eternity."

I cringed and waited for their response. Black parents do not take to cosmic thinking. I waited, counting on my mother to be the one to either get up and loudly exit the room or simply lunge at him. But it was my father's tart response that caught me off guard.

"Well, sir, you are going to need more than whatever bullshit that was you just said to raise a family and make it in this world, especially given I hear you play music for a living."

Lord, I thought, *he wasted no time.* I detected a subtle smile on my mother's face as she backed him up with a "That's right" followed by her long-perfected eye roll and low-pitched "*humph.*" After an only slightly less strained meal and conversation, Daniel and I sped back up I-25 to Denver, had a dinner lightly eaten, then moved on with our lives with only a faint blessing from my family.

We navigated our way through a beautiful life season before separating, mostly for practical reasons. Daniel went on the road touring, and I knew that was the right path for him, but no place for me and a baby. Once Ian arrived, serious mothering began. I moved closer to my parents so they could help me with Ian while I finished grad school and worked.

Life indeed presented itself as a barrier to Daniel's and my vision of being world changers together, metaphysically, and musically, but the three of us stayed very close. Ian developed a sweet and poignant relationship with his father, and they shared a love of art, secrets, a glistening gap-toothed smile, and identical hands with long, delicate, and graceful fingers.

When Daniel passed away years later, answers came rushing to me as to why our lives had transpired as they had. He was a creative force, a golden thread to hold fast to, for Ian to hold fast to. It was apparent to Daniel, and he mirrored back to me, that I always came back to music. This meant I gravitated to people who shared my way of seeing the world, artistically, aesthetically, creatively. Music allowed for an even bigger vision of impacting the world, of leaving the world better, a saying my father frequently used long before it coincidentally was a mantra at Apple. Music opened my mind to seeing the beauty of the human spirit, the artistry of every situation.

Staying connected to my creative life was necessary for my personal thriving, and it messaged something important to others around me, even in the workplace to employees. Some colleagues told me it inspired them to rebalance their lives with pursuits they loved and excelled at, or wanted to excel at. Others simply said it was a calming, steadying force.

My strategy of performing while working was restorative. It offered a barrier of protection to my soul when I needed it. In lieu of living solely in service to corporate mandates, I understood how to extract from my work what most inspired me, then direct my energy toward that inspiration, in the same way one does when performing a piece, a role, an aria.

With every new Apple Store built, or a new operational process, I needed to find how, in the scheme of it all, the work was important to a bigger vision. Initially in my career I did this for my own self-preservation. But at a certain point I realized approaching it this way did get at the essence of the intersection of technology and humanity. In the day-to-day, find what gives you a surge of energy. Hint: You're already probably navigating your days in this direction. Certain people, activities. The way you think or problem-solve or laugh when you spend time with some more so than others. The impracticality of this guidance is less than you might initially see. Interspersing our days with the people or activities that offer energy or inspiration only requires some planning, and even if it is one hour or less of any given day, it is of value. In turn, being more mindful about becoming more of that kind of an energy source for others suddenly shifts the equation as well. An entire group or team thinking this way can turn a culture from flat to fun, from tedious to mutually enjoyable. It is why the staff loved so much of the work my team was responsible for at Apple; it presented constant opportunities for mutuality, to see something we could positively impact, learn from, impart to.

I was fortunate to have been one of a team of talented individuals leading the global Apple Stores. It was a fascinating collection of people with a common thread: a belief that pretty much anything could be accomplished when you held fast to a vision, but the vision wholly involved the energy and talent of people. Envisioning the gathering of all kinds of people, to experience technology in the form of Apple products, to be transformed by everything about that experience, from the brilliance of the design to the intuitive thoughtfulness and capabilities of the product (all envisioned by people). Then simultaneously enhancing how people learned about technology, while diminishing our fears of it. It was humbling and powerful, and it was surprisingly people centered.

Over the course of writing this book I have listened to brilliant people talk about the moments when they felt the most seen, who had "seen" them, and most important, why it mattered, what it meant, what they took forward from it. When we are seen, it is often a reverse roadmap of cues that unfolded throughout our lives. Those times when we were seen tell us much about who we are at a very core level. My hope is that we can recall those times, replant them prominently in our lives, and allow them to inform and teach us more about the person sitting, standing, living, working next to us—in time for it to be useful.

Bernard Tyson was the chief executive officer of Kaiser Permanente and one of the few Black CEOs in America. Presiding over health care for twelve million people, he was highly regarded, and beloved in the communities in which he operated. He died of a heart attack in early November of 2019, after many of us had seen him just days prior at a Museum of the African Diaspora fundraiser in San Francisco.

Bernard and I had been longtime members of the Executive Leadership Council (ELC), a membership organization exclusively for Black C-suite executives and board-level directors. Bernard's memorial services were held at Chase Center in San Francisco, home of the Golden State Warriors and a stunning and sizable event center. The floor level of the arena was full, front to back. At a point in the ceremony, one of the singers on stage led the stadium in singing "Lean on Me." And in that moment, this collection of Black leaders and executives, hundreds strong, sang together, in full choir voices, "Lean on me . . . when you're not strong, and I'll be your friend, I'll help you carry on, for, it won't be long, till I'm gonna need somebody to lean on."

In that powerful moment of celebrating Mr. Tyson's life, I wondered how many of these brilliant, impressive leaders in Fortune 500 companies might have had the same experiences I did, learning much about how life worked from the pews of churches, baseball fields, piano recitals, sidewalk play, dinner table conversations, and nurturing communities they'd grown up in. Threading together the meaningful moments where they were *seen,* moments that changed the course of their lives, that parlayed them into becoming some of the most powerful leaders in the country. Because in that moment it sounded as though we'd all traveled a similar path. Every voice was on message. That message? We are here, sharing a common moment. Here, of course, to celebrate a fallen colleague, to see him all the way through his journey. But gathered here also to mobilize how we will go forward. Seeing one another, as that is our power. Enriching. Empowering. Being seen, being heard. Recognizing this process as the will of our ancestors.

Chapter 6

I Am Not Your Numbers

I wish I could say
all the things I should say,
say 'em loud, say 'em clear
for the whole round world to hear.

—NINA SIMONE, "I WISH I KNEW
HOW IT WOULD FEEL TO BE FREE"

I began my Apple journey in Fountain, Colorado. I had heard that Apple had a new presence just ten miles south of where I was living, and one night, while out dining with friends, I met one of the new senior managers of the facility. He encouraged me to interview. I admitted to not knowing a lot about Apple, but I knew the company had a "cool" reputation (that is, it was not IBM, Digital Equipment Corporation, or HP). I knew it had a rainbow logo and was loved by schools. I was peripherally aware of Steve Jobs's publicized departure from the company back in 1985 but didn't pay a ton of attention to who was currently running things, ten years later.

Even then, Apple's rep of creativity and coolness prevailed. Friends more familiar with the company locally spoke about self-directed work teams, and how the high-tech, product-producing facility felt less like a production plant and more like a hub of cutting-edge research and development. They spoke of the headquarters in Cupertino, California, as though it were a mythical place. Intrigued, I followed up and interviewed with them. *Why not?* I thought. While I appreciated the work I was doing and the mentorship of J. Brown, there was something very appealing about working for a tech company focused on enabling students, educators, designers, and thinkers.

Here was a company putting technology in the hands of a community of creators. In meeting with them, I believed there could be much more human engagement in the work they were doing in the world, given what they were already doing (even though the iPhone and its mode of mobile computing hadn't yet been dreamed up).

Apple hired me as a college and community recruiting specialist to help them acclimate and find good local talent in the Colorado community where they'd built this offsite operation. Hiring me locally was a way to better understand the region, and was a significant investment into this unique community they basically knew little about. It was a cost-effective move, relocating production to lower cost markets, but where there was an existing talent pool. I like to think I gave them that street cred in the local area, as we were able to hire the facility to capacity and produce prolifically.

The Colorado Apple site was the company's second largest production site in the world, yet felt like its own entity—a close-knit, well-run operations site, focused on physically building the products of its era: Power Macs and PowerBooks. It was wholly operational, and most of us who worked there were at earlier stages of our careers and seemingly worlds away from Apple HQ in Cupertino, California.

With new corporate leadership in place, in 1997 Apple divested the Colorado site. Like most everyone at the site, I

was soon to be unemployed. But a few days after the announcement, I received a phone call from Cupertino, asking
me to consider moving there for a job. Apple was offering me
a new role in employee relations, the department that advocates for the voice of employees.

I was a little stunned. There was no formal interview process, so I'd never seen this offer coming and was totally unpre-
pared to consider it. "You want me to pick up my family and
move to the most expensive place on earth?" It turned out
that along with me, several other employees and their families
had been recommended to be "saved" and relocated to Cupertino.

I was doing fine where I was, living comfortably and af-
fordably back in Colorado, in the community I had grown up
in and knew well. Now I was suddenly faced with a huge decision: stay safe and comfortable in Colorado or take a leap of
faith and enter yet another different world.

I've always had a strong sense of intuition. I was never a
plod-through-life kind of person, but always tried to see the
meaning and purpose in things, the bigger vision for my life.

For me, "bigger" meant I had the responsibility to see what
I could do for others around me and coming after me—others
without my advantages, without my committed family and
community. With values passed to me from my dad, and a way
of living that was the simple and singular truth of my upbringing. I saw that a move to Northern California, and this new
job, had potential to make a real difference. It could offer opportunities artistically for my son; we'd be exposed to more
diverse cultures, music, people. I saw the opportunity to expand, and that helped make it an easy decision.

I had visited Cupertino once before when invited to Apple

HQ for an annual HR conference. It was a big deal to be invited, and it was my first insight into what I saw as tech culture's inclusive exclusivity—the experience of being both "in" and "out" with no clear understanding of how you'd arrived there. I was inside of one group yet excluded from another; constantly. And it was a pattern that would be oft repeated. I suppose that is life in general, but tech certainly has a way of making it more pronounced.

At the conference, I was overwhelmed by a feeling of *everyone in this room is smart and is going to let you know it*. At the same time, that did not necessarily feel like a bad thing. There seemed to be something important to that message. Despite this feeling, it was my first experience of being around more than a sprinkling of colleagues of color, and an immediate sense of belonging came over me. We barely had time to meet one another, but just their presence, the knowledge that I was far from an "only" in that room, made a difference. I felt like an outsider because of my geography, not because of my skin color or gender—that was a first.

When the conference keynote speaker Santiago Rodriguez took the stage, I was mesmerized. He began talking about building a truly diverse and multicultural workforce, and it was the first time I'd heard these ideas laid out with such vision, presented with a "we'd all win" attitude that sounded so compelling and attainable. It was also the first time I heard the concept of a diverse workforce described with no reference to "affirmative action."

For years of my working life, affirmative action and the Equal Employment Opportunity Commission's principles and regulations were attached to me wherever I went. As necessary as these laws were at the time, there was the resentment of their default association to constantly contend with. A backlash residual that awaited us at every turn, always waiting to remind anyone who differed from a dominant white straight male profile that we were there because of a policy, and not merit. And now, here before me was this resplendent Latino man, elegant, unapologetic, candid about matters of race, and completely detaching the concepts of rich representation from the "we have to hire you because you are Black, female, etc." I asked the people around me, "Who *is* this man?"

For those who thought the diversity in technology conversations were new to these last couple of decades, Santiago was director of multicultural programs at Apple in the late 1990s. His words still resonate as the most progressive I have ever heard in a business setting. His work focused on the value of everyone's cultural and individual uniqueness, at a time, more than twenty-five years ago, when few leaders and companies were even talking about this, let alone making it a business priority. Santiago set out to change that. He was no-nonsense, commanding, a force. When you heard him speak, he challenged the mind and inspired the soul, yet his words felt tangible, his ideas actionable. I was both jolted and moved by his words—words and ideas that people are still grappling with today, as DEI, known today as Diversity, Equity and Inclusion, yet again faces classic backlash as it is recast as an enemy of men.

I tried to secure a meeting with Santiago, but he was a VIP, and my short visit to Cupertino did not allow me to work into his schedule. But I "followed" him (not on social media, which did not yet exist as we now know it) and with some determination secured copies of his speeches and requested his taped video talks. I finally met him when I returned to Cupertino and attended a workshop he led. He was gracious, yet even more resolute in person, suffering no fools when it came to the importance of this work.

Sadly, Santiago left Apple later that year for a role at Microsoft, just after I had made the move to California. He died a short time later, in 2000. It was a huge loss for the diversity movement and practitioners. His ideas had helped me realize that not enough people even understand the core meaning of the diverse representation that he spoke of so radically. He illuminated how the concepts of diversity and inclusion were different and not interchangeable, separating the conversation even more distinctly from the affirmative action debate. He positioned it all as simple business and talent savvy, rather than a mandated bureaucratic burden, and this was very new talk for business people. Santiago enlightened leaders on the *tragedy* of exclusion—tragic because the real losses of excluding people are economical, psychological, sociological, representing significant loss to business and to the whole of humanity.

When I heard Santiago for the very first time, I believed that in some small way I would help carry on his mission at Apple and in the world. I believed I would do this on my own terms; certainly not as something called a diversity leader, but simply as myself. As it turns out, I did exactly that—although the road there was never easy.

In 1996 my family settled into a townhome in a Campbell suburb and started to become acclimated to the dynamics of Northern California. I was delighted to travel up and down the peninsula to local art and music festivals, and to my first California Juneteenth, celebrated full throttle in Evergreen Valley Park in San Jose. Our Juneteenths in Colorado were family tradition. Ian, at ten, had sold his very first pieces of art at the annual celebration: a Bob Marley sketch and a calendar of Black family scenes. Juneteenth was a special celebration for us, wonderfully free of commercialization until many years later, after George Floyd's murder.

At Apple, I was immediately welcomed by Black colleagues who were dialed in to a network of African American professionals, families, and companies in the area. Employee resource groups were newly forming at the time, and those of us who made up what was then called the African American Employees Association (now titled Black@Apple) were a reliable source of connection. There was a kind of secret Black bat signal beamed up among professionals in the area, and I immediately met mid- and high-level Black colleagues from HP, Silicon Graphics, Netscape, Atari, Yahoo, and many more.

The various meet-and-greets almost felt like an HBCU gathering: You had a place to belong, a place to be; you fit somewhere. It felt this way because the individuals who made up this Black tech community were people who decided to see others, not ignore them. There was value in what we all had to offer, not competition. Looking back, I think somehow we knew no one but us would do this for us. I also believe we knew these were precious connections that could be lost once we became more entrenched in our respective companies.

Today, these types of gatherings feel even more urgent, even necessary. Research from professor Laura Morgan Roberts of the University of Virginia's Darden School of Business found that professionals of color are at higher risk of becoming isolated at work and struggle to navigate the racial boundaries at social events, which impedes their ability to forge deep relationships. As employees of color, we have to lead the process of networking, ensuring we know one another. Our ability to thrive is profoundly aided by the connection, knowledge, and influence we share.

At that time, the Bay Area had an abundance of opportunity for those savvy enough to know to be there and fortunate enough to have found a way to do so. Between this newfound community of successful people of color and what I quickly discovered was also a welcoming artistic community, I knew I'd found my new extended home.

What I did not know, and would not learn for years, was that Blacks had lived in, worked in, and contributed significantly to Silicon Valley for over half a century, at large tech companies, as entrepreneurs, as scholars and researchers. Just as my Colorado community's history held untold stories about "invisible" Black pioneers, cowboys, artists, settlers, miners, craftspeople, and business leaders, the rich history of Blacks in technology was also not broadly known, and we were again unseen—as remains the case today.

As I made the Valley my home, technology and private equity investment came together to grow social networking technologies, billion-dollar unicorn companies, and phenomenally profitable enterprises. This would all make an undeniable imprint on the world, yet we saw or heard little about Black people in these stories of wealth creation, innovation, creativity, and world-changing research.

Somehow our footprint became smaller, opportunities phased out, our presence diminished. The historical exclusion Black people are accustomed to exists abundantly in technology, and the absence and silence of our involvement in the advent of big tech further fuels the narrative around our absence in tech today. Yet, we *were* there. We were excluded from entrepreneurial and investment opportunities and circles. We were rarely included in the clubby worlds of startups and stock equity. We were here. Programming, leading, managing, creating, innovating.

Filmmaker Kathy Cotton set out to elevate this narrative in her documentary *A Place at the Table: The Story of the African American Pioneers of Silicon Valley,* which highlights the astoundingly talented and smart people within "Black Valley"—a term coined by HBCU-Apple-Microsoft intern Paul Hammond. Despite being inside major technology firms, we know well the stories of so many people of color being unseen, ignored, dismissed, and blocked from access to VC funding.

Despite these challenges, one of the best practices of Black Valley was lauding each other's achievements: PhDs, promotions, children accepted into schools, new jobs, career and life milestones. And when someone was seen, when that promotion or funding opportunity did happen, word reverberated through *our* Valley. If only the financial rewards had followed, we'd have forged a formidable tech presence, and I can't help but wonder how much more robust, vibrant, and "seeing" the tech sector story might have been.

I have now lived and worked in the Valley for decades, and inequities and exclusion still exist. A study by the Silicon Valley Institute for Regional Studies stated that the wealth and inequality gap was so compelling that if Silicon Valley were a country, the wealth disparity would be considered politically unstable. Forty-six percent of children living amid the wealth of Silicon Valley currently live in households that are not self-sufficient, requiring publicly funded support. When those who have lived and worked there and benefited from the tech sector's dominance are able to just ignore these stark realities, it is not surprising that the call for diversity and representation in tech that I heard from a visionary twenty-five years ago remains the same call to action we hear today.

When I moved to Cupertino, no company publicized statistics of compositional diversity, but I can tell you the names of the top female Black leaders then, and I can cite them now. Black women leading anything in technology was going to be a short list. In 2021, Salesforce, after significant criticism, began an initiative to "address microaggressions in the workplace." This startling statement all but admitted a multitude of issues in one sentence, as the company grappled with new trainings and initiatives. One Black female employee posted on LinkedIn: "Have you ever smiled and cried at the same time?" as she tendered her very public resignation. And Black women across the platform felt her anguish personally resonate. It matters not if we are tech leaders, university presidents, supreme court justices, mayors of sanctuary cities, Amazon or DoorDash drivers, call center or nursing staff . . . the anguish of Black women remains universal.

In 2021, out of 30,745 workers in professional roles, Apple employed 177 Black women, or less than 1 percent. At many of the tables where I and other Black leaders in tech companies sat, these small numbers—2, 4, or even 6 percent—were discussed as problematic, but not, I thought, for the right reasons. They were addressing the numbers, not the people those numbers represented. From my vantage point there was no delving into the experiences those small numbers were having, only their existence as statistics.

For the entirety of my time leading in technology, there was much handwringing in leadership circles over its lack of diversity, yet leaders chronically failed to recognize why this was. They missed the fact that I and other employees of color were not statistics. Diversity discussions and mandates turned us into one-dimensional integers that did not represent actual people, families, and communities. No mutuality exists or is extended, therefore insight is limited. One-way relationships are typically sight-impaired.

My colleagues across the Valley complained about being trotted out for photographs for Black History Month or a product launch video, or to create a faux setting for the latest diversity materials. I rarely heard of gatherings where our thoughts, feelings, or ideas were solicited as part of the process of utilizing our images. When such meetings did happen, there was often a heavy presence of company "editors" whose job it was to ensure that nothing uncomfortable or controversial arose from meeting with employees, with people—the very people being charted about, analyzed, and "problem solved."

Many of the conversations I was aware of across the Valley focused on external appearances. What kind of judgment would these representation numbers evoke, and from whom? What would be said or written? Who would read, who would care? Both the companies and the media failed to consider that by having these superficial internal conversations, followed by publicly minimizing and explaining away the numbers, we were being told we were invisible, unseen numerically and physically. Yes, we were small in numbers, but we still existed.

If even one of the more influential tech companies had considered how to meaningfully engage with its own BIPOC, what might have happened? Perhaps these companies would have come to understand the experiences of the people of color already there and contributing day to day. I knew that more discussion directly with us about what could possibly change could prove fruitful, albeit uncomfortable and frequently painful to hear. How many leaders are ready to hear information that challenges their beliefs about themselves and requires accountability for a non-repeating future? Which messengers might be shot? Likely the wrong ones, the most informative ones as my colleagues and I bore witness to.

I took advantage of a booming dot-com era, walking away from Apple in its conflicted era of rotating chief executives and confusing product offerings, prior to Steve Jobs's return in 2000. It was a confident move on my part, as I felt capable of navigating the greater Silicon Valley despite having been there only a little over a year. The move was also indicative of how dynamic and lucrative this time was, as the NASDAQ index grew by 400 percent and new "internet" companies launched weekly.

I took a jaunt farther north of Cupertino onto famed Sand Hill Road and lived among the "unicorns," becoming HR director for a well-funded startup that developed the first technology for airline and travel reservation engines. In other words, the earliest form of Travelocity, prior to its acquisition by Sabre Travel Corporation. The concept disintermediated travel agencies, and I was there for the initial conversations and agreements with the primary participating airlines—United, Lufthansa, and eventually other Star Alliance partners.

In mythical startup fashion, within the walls of our offices, the founders of the technology skateboarded through the building and rode motorcycles home at night—when they actually went home. Staff meetings were spontaneous, programmers were entitled, donuts were the preferred office currency, and people slept and lived in corners and nooks of the building, assuring boundaries problematically breached. Entire families worked together, and one birthday celebration included a lace thong as a gift from one of the founders. My job was to convert all this into a working startup, viable, behaving, and poised for either an initial public offering (IPO) with Goldman Sachs or a sale to the highest bidder.

I treated it as an adventure. I was a Wonder Woman battling to protect the new technology concept as it found its way into the mainstream, which it eventually did. And for a season, it was an odd sort of comic book fun—until it wasn't. Me being me, I longed for some semblance of infrastructure, for serious mindedness. I quickly tired of one more environment where people were "othered," but this time because they didn't have a high enough tolerance for the absurd.

Hardly anyone I knew believed my stories of life between Page Mill and Sand Hill Road in Palo Alto, so I kept most of them to myself. The lesson for me was that people could as readily find ways to exclude others in chaos and confusion as in order and routine.

As a result of my work in this world, however, I was called upon frequently to consult with a select few venture capital investors on the caliber of their portfolio talent. I contributed to an IPO and an acquisition, and I had my first experiences with viable employee stock equity and a rising stock price. We bought a modest house and the car I'd long hoped to drive, and suddenly had fewer worries for Ian's college funding.

Then I received a surprising call. "You need to come back;

we need you," said my former colleague at Apple, almost in a whisper. "You really should come back. Steve is coming back permanently. Things are going to be happening." When we'd hung up, I just stared at the phone.

Steve had indeed returned. He'd sold NeXT, the company he started after leaving Apple, returning now as an advisor, even interim CEO, and ultimately sitting squarely back in the seat of chief—and moving well along on the all-too-short journey that changed Apple and the world forever.

Six weeks after that phone call, I found myself back at the company, in a position I'd always wanted, directing employee relations worldwide. I was eager to dig into the job because I saw the opportunity to positively impact how employees were seen and heard. Now I could help build the kind of culture I'd always wanted to be a part of.

Within the HR populations of companies, employee relations (ER) work is intriguing to only a few who understand it and do it well. It is thankless, invisible, intense, but always fascinating, given its proximity to the core of how people live and work together. Companies with strong ER departments count on them to handle grievances, investigate allegations, enforce employee conduct, and mitigate liability, but that is only part of the job.

I saw the work more broadly. I believed the ER department should serve as a voice and conduit to employees, as a barometer of healthy culture or first indicator of the need for developing better leadership. I saw the work as human complexity problems to solve and learn from, to incorporate ways to being better, more effective, to study and know who the best leaders were and why. To learn more about the kinds of environments and cultural nuances that would encourage failures rather than punish for missteps or mistakes. I was excited to do ER work differently—to pull it out of punitive basements, bunkers, and dim cubicles, where it lived in a red zone of liability, where the dark and difficult stories went to be dismantled and buried.

In time I realized we could bring light to dark corridors by enacting policies allowing people to be heard and seen, whether through better-constructed performance reviews, more objective investigations, and the hiring of an ER team who did not see employees as inherently problematic. People stumble daily in work situations. An assurance that no matter what transpired, they would be heard, seemed to just be smart business, giving way to better resolutions and often more amicable departures.

My team was a group of professional investigators, interviewers, data analysts, and lawyers. We'd all experienced the ungratifying outcomes of merely addressing the "what" of a situation, so we made every attempt to operate with a "why?" and "how did we get here?" philosophy. The "what happened" of a matter, in all its intricate detail, was a compelling enough exercise. It was always surprising to me how much effort went into understanding every detail of the "what," before a bullet fast-forwarding to solutions. But the "why" of the matter got us so much further. Why is this situation occurring, and continuously? What have you been told about why your proposals have not been considered? Why do you believe you're being overlooked for this promotion? Why is there this much friction between these department leaders?

I enjoyed the "whys." People will absolutely tell you their thoughts as to why, and there is almost always substance to their observations, we just had to assess and evaluate them.

More facts would reveal themselves, more useful information always came to bear.

I loved this time of my career: head down, working diligently to enhance and improve human experiences. Steve and his team of gifted technologists—including chief product designer Jony Ive; Avie Tevanian, principal software designer of the Mac operating system; chief hardware leader Jon Rubenstein; and, recruited later, iPod designer Tony Fadell—were reshaping the products and the company. Steve was gifted at many things, but his passion was indeed not for the milquetoast, the faint of heart, or the noncommittal. He was adamant about great talent and made talent acquisition and recruiting a prominent function.

In this era, the culture at Apple, with its driven, demanding, exacting cycles, led to product excellence of the highest order. I watched people make personal and professional decisions to serve that high order, while everything else within their personal ecosystem took a functional place, to allow full capacity to serve the call. One new executive likened it to entering a monastery, another to a military branch. For those of us who would accompany Steve on this leg of the Apple journey, so many of us had an ability to see. As I recall, users and customers also began to say they felt seen too.

In my work I tried to take a similar approach, expecting people to rise to what I saw in them, and offering a vision of themselves they could rally around. I pulled heavily from my family's dinner table lessons to establish that same philosophy around what really mattered and mattered for people. I saw this simply as a level of personal dignity and respect—that caught people off guard. They just did not expect it, were not accustomed to being listened to, seen, respected, especially when they were bringing forward an issue.

My longtime assistant, Karl Miller, a man skilled at observation, would often observe, "People come into your office with a cloud, a frown, and heaviness, and I rarely ever see them leave with it. They always leave differently." That was important to hear, and beyond just complimentary, it stood as proof I was true to my own vision for myself. It was not validation I'd hear from leadership, not how they'd quantify success, but how I did.

I was in my role in ER for only a year when the senior vice president of HR, Dan Walker, tapped me on the shoulder and said, "We've got this little project that we're building. Keep doing what you're doing, but we'd really like you to also come and help us out and get some things set up." That little project turned out to be a massive ground-up effort to build out the soon-to-be-revealed Apple Stores, putting all its operational and cultural infrastructure in place.

We'd meet in confidential places and buildings, different groups focused in different areas—marketing, merchandising, real estate, recruiting—doing unprecedented and amazing thinking and planning. Because I felt firmly esconced in my ER job, and rather liked it, I remember going back to Dan and saying, "So, I think this is going to be a big deal, and I think you should get someone to permanently be the head of the people aspects of it and run with this Store thing."

And he said, simply, "Okay." At that moment I forgot that the person I was speaking to was a legendary master of talent, who had built multiple companies, including Gap Inc., by wholly understanding how to optimize people and their skills. I had no idea at that time I was the laser focus of his intent.

Several people were looked at for the position, both internally and externally. Dan circled back to me and said, "I've talked to a bunch of people, and we'd like you to take this job." I said no at first, because I was a little intimidated, honestly, as I knew little of how retailing really worked.

I said, "Look, I've grown up in certain types of industries and feel like I know those. Despite being a consummate shoe shopper, I really know nothing about the business of retailing. I just don't readily get it."

And Dan, in his wisdom, said, "But you know people and you know culture, and you know it better than anyone else that we've met or that we know inside of the company, period, bar none."

From the earliest stages, the very first executive hired to envision and lead the Apple Stores, Ron Johnson, wanted to build something that led with people, so the customer experience could always closely intersect with the products. Dan understood my desire to connect ER issues to leadership capability throughout the company. Everything begins and ends with a leader, the tone she or he sets, and the culture they create. It was clear that I saw things through the same human lens that Ron did—we were a matched business pairing fueled by the same belief in prioritizing the souls of the people.

As gratifying as it was to be acknowledged in this way, I also hoped they'd singled me out for the right reasons of competency. It was a coveted position, and lots of people wanted it, including headline-grabbing outsiders and Apple highfliers who openly stated they thought they were better suited for the role, or more deserving of it.

I took the role, hoping that these two renowned retailing visionaries would look back and say, "We made the right choice—she 'got' it."

I saw Ron Johnson and Dan Walker as much like my other early "seers." As I grew to know them, I believed that long term they would support me in the important ways, and they did. My requirements of support were remarkably simple: to be seen and acknowledged, to be treated fairly and respectfully, and to share access to information and exchange insight. For my part, I was already educated and seasoned in the use of empathy and leading with humanity, and I had, for years, believed in the power of both to ensure successful outcomes. I now had a new opportunity to show up and lean into myself. The rest became history.

Chapter 7

Your Presence Is Requested But May Be Ignored

I met a woman long ago,
her hair the black that black can go.
Are you a teacher of the heart?
Soft, she answered no.

—LEONARD COHEN, "TEACHERS"

Despite their proud, prominent heritage, and declarations of equity following the events of 2020, the community of America's HBCUs remains largely unseen by corporate America. Howard University, Morehouse, Spelman College, and a handful of others are exceptions. I've often had to educate others about the existence of my own alma mater, Grambling State University; spell out the acronym of HBCU; and explain the whole of education for Black people in post–Civil War America. A few memorable lines from those conversations:

"I've never heard of it. It must be a private school." No, it is a public, state-funded university that has existed for over a century.

"Oh, is it accredited?" One would think so, given it is government funded, but yes, it holds many accreditations.

"I have heard of a few of those schools. I didn't know they still existed; why are they needed?" There are still significant barriers to education for Black students and other groups, especially in the parts of the country that embraced enslavement.

"Why did you choose to go there, you were very smart!" Brilliant kids choose to or opt to attend predominantly Black colleges and universities. It may be a matter of access or affordability but also cultural preference.

"Oh ..." not waiting until the end of my statements and moving on quickly to the next topic.

When I was first recruited for a job at Apple, it was apparent to me that the tech industry at large had little understanding of the significance of Black colleges. A few HBCUs may have stood out for their well-known alumni: Dr. Martin Luther King, director Spike Lee as Morehouse College alum; author Toni Morrison, actor Chad Boseman, or Supreme Court Justice Thurgood Marshall all Howard University alumni. A handful of historical stories are known about very few HBCUs. For example, Wilberforce University in Ohio (the first college to be owned and operated by Black people, founded by the African Methodist Episcopalian Church and ultimately a cultural center for the Black elite), or Fisk University in Tennessee known for its famed Fisk Jubilee Singers, an award-winning a cappella group that has been awarded a National Medal of Arts. In its early years of touring the singers traveled the path of the Underground Railroad and eventually pulled the university out of financial loss. Perhaps some had heard of my alum Grambling University because of its prominent football program, producing some of the greatest names on NFL team rosters, or its world-renowned marching band, which appeared in six Super Bowl halftimes. Maybe a handful had even heard of Spelman as a college of distinction for Black women; Tuskeegee University, educational home of the celebrated WWII Tuskegee Airmen; or Florida A&M, the largest public HBCU that sits on a campus that was formerly a slave plantation owned by a Florida governor.

Examine the list of 102 HBCUs and it reads like a Smithsonian exhibit of history, legacy, and stories of excellence, survival, and of thriving while America struggled to establish its equilibrium and get onto its feet. At some point I took on fewer of these conversations and private history lessons (recommending the reading of articles instead). But I continued to interact with people who sat in roles of critical responsibility, roles of access, roles that unlocked doors for talent who simply had zero awareness of this particular community of talent. I saw it as my professional leadership responsibility to educate them on the statistics of HBCU graduates, the untapped talent pool of HBCU students, and how talented people of color were not afforded the same access or opportunities to attend schools considered premier in technology and HBCUs were relied upon to fill those gaps. This water was mine to carry for at least a decade in tech until other HBCU grads permeated more of tech culture and took up the task with me, picking up more and more buckets along the way, which was precisely the way it felt. Like carrying water buckets.

That first recruiter I ever spoke to at Apple in 1994 advised me, as I moved through my interview process, to reorder my résumé to not lead with my college degree from an HBCU. He recommended I highlight my "life and professional experience." It was clear that school pedigree was a thing he cared about and believed others did too. And though he clearly saw me as a viable candidate, it was just not on the merits of my education. With good intentions, he attempted to "protect" me from being dismissed or deprioritized before the full hiring team could meet me in person. In that sense, he "saw" me. I gave him the benefit of the doubt because he made an effort to lead the process with me the person, rather than my résumé, even if for interesting reasons of his lack of awareness of the prevalence or prominence of Black colleges.

Also interesting in my initial Apple interaction was the use of the term "life experience," an ofttimes coded-language term used to describe women taking time away to have and care for children, people of color experiencing challenging and frequent bouts of unemployment, or older applicants with deep expertise passed over for not being "hungry" or "fresh" enough. These process flaws were tough concepts for white male hiring teams to grasp, and for whom paths to meaningful opportunities were not as fraught. I look back and realize I myself was a highly unlikely hire, on face value. Someone, or a few someones, had to have seen something about me they thought had merit. Overall, for many years, hiring in technology was a fascinating study on biased tracking of applicants and how human touch outcomes—varied, inconsistent— impacted a company's demographics. More robust applicant tracking systems, debiasing applicant tracking software, and improved interviewing practices all help. But the work of writing this book, and the work of trying to point colleagues in right directions, included spending countless hours scouring for solutions that might move things along. I'd chase down the promise of a "study" only to find it and have it tell me what I knew already: That companies believe their improvement intentions are enough even as these same intentions have already proven insufficient. Headlong into the AI era, companies are already underestimating the impact of AI now entrusted to "diversify," "monitor," and "audit," all while their algorithms have been optimized for the dominant groups that created them. And although the current reports tell us that soon AI will possess emotional intelligence, who are the current possessors of that skill, that wisdom, and are they in the right rooms yet? Or is this underrepresented as well, because the skills of empathy, awareness of othering, and engagement rest in greater abundance within the people not yet represented in digital creation—women and BIPOC? Sean Celli, a friend and longtime talent acquisition strategist, for years stayed at the forefront of understanding the criticality of debiasing the recruitment process, its technology, and the big business ecosystem that impedes it. "We aren't very far along," he admitted when I reached out. Having sat at tops of multiple companies' talent functions and implemented multiple interventions, he knows all too well that outcomes will continue to look exactly as they do without a change of course. When the stats and demographics we have experienced in the tech industry for years have been largely due to dismal representation, abundant bias, and cultural incompetence, and when even the best in the business have to acknowledge that little change has occurred, we can be assured that we are not building a digitally inclusive future, but instead facing down even more exclusive and *unseeing* outcomes for our services and products. Business leaders will continue contributing to the chasm, when they could, instead, and with their tremendous assets, power, and wealth, reimagine and reengineer how we engage with talent. They could, as Steve Jobs once did, make an in-the-moment decision in the cafeteria to do something different, unprecedented. They could decide to mutually learn from Black interns on campus versus count them. They could visit at least one of America's HBCUs and try to understand how to incorporate some of their resilience. They could make investments, not contributions. They could behave radically, urgently, courageously against backlash. They could decide to see.

In the early years of building teams for the Apple Stores, we tried to represent the communities the Stores existed in. In markets like New York, Atlanta, and Southern California, this gleaned some representation for the company at large, later reflected in diversity reporting. It also meant the Store teams initially reflected much of the company's overall representation. This was actually a good story, though the media seemed to want to make it a flaw, a "low wage" story instead of a potentially exciting pipeline story.

The Stores represented a new talent stream the company could develop and leverage. Long before it became a media issue, our Apple Store leaders were innovating ways to move new talent around, offering them "experiences" that would ultimately make them attractive within various store markets, across the company or the broader job market. It became a badge of honor to say you worked in an Apple Store. Store staff who departed for better jobs were well trained and primed with experiences that would serve them in new jobs, and they were "clapped out," applauded and sent off with a celebration. For years, the Apple Stores boasted some of the lowest attrition in the retail industry. Part of the appeal was a culture where staff understood how to see, value, and include others. The most frequent anecdotal statement we heard from employees? "I feel like I belong here." The most frequently quantified testimony from employees? "I would recommend working here to my friends and family."

When we opened the first Apple Stores in Atlanta in 2002, we engaged with the very prominent HBCU community in Atlanta to recruit for positions. Spelman. Morehouse. Clark. Morris Brown. Spelman had a world-class robotics team. Clark had an outstanding film production department. And despite years of operational issues, Morris Brown was known for distinguished alumni such as civil rights activist Hosea Williams and Beverly Harvard, the first Black female police chief of Atlanta. Our visits to HBCUs came at least a decade before this approach became a popular formulaic way for companies to seek Black talent. My team and I believed in the marketplace cachet of an Apple work opportunity, yet we were met with skepticism from Black faculty, parents, and students.

"Why?" they said, "when we have worked so hard to send our children to our HBCUs, Morehouse, Spelman . . . why would you want us to think working at some retail store in the mall is a good idea for our students?"

I explained. Apple provided real-time business education. It offered exposure to leading technology products. There was an opportunity to learn about leadership in a multimillion-dollar-generating technology operation with sales, service, and education offerings. It was not counting jeans or sunglasses; it was a full-breadth business experience.

I was able to speak of my own experience. As an HBCU graduate, I had risen to executive levels at the world's most admired tech company. What I said to them I said with sincerity and integrity. I made this community aware that I understood these were special students, with incredible insights to offer to a company. They were savvy early adopters and trend setters, and I knew that within this culture I'd cocreated, these students had every potential to learn, grow, be truly seen, and advance their experiences into rich careers if they wanted to do so.

In the space of a forty-five-minute presentation, we translated our proposition to this rightfully protective, skeptical community of parents and academic stewards who reminded me of my aunts, uncles, and HBCU faculty. Without my cultural understanding of this audience, our recruiting team may have walked away from the opportunity and left with zero relationship traction with a very important community of customers and future employees. But I had been one of them; I had seen and understood their concerns, and knew them to be warranted, in a way others missed. This community of parents and professors saw their own students and their value and recognized the mutual value in the relationship. This is a lesson of DEI work. It is not a one-way street or charity-donation opportunity for people of color. I wished that the tech community could have witnessed the diligence of the schools and parents as they queried us, "Why should we allow our precious students to be recruited into a company that has not extended itself to us, not seen us, not understood *our* value?" I wished that picture could have replaced the one I was so familiar with: of impoverished students standing outside looking in, clamoring to become a part of our shiny tech world.

During this process, I met and befriended Dr. Andrew Williams, a Spelman engineering professor and founder of the school's award-winning women's robotics team, the SpelBots. Dr. Williams was brilliant, compassionate, fun, and devoted to student learning experiences. My colleagues and I were immediately enamored with him and the group of stunningly talented students he led. We invited him to Cupertino, just because we wanted to continue the relationship, and because we enjoyed him. We wanted others to know about him, his students, and his program, and potentially bring it into the awareness of our engineering teams.

About a year later, Dr. Williams did come out to visit Apple's famed Infinite Loop campus. A group of us took him to lunch at Café Mac. Almost as if scripted, Steve walked by. Dr. Williams walked directly over to him and told him of his love for all things Apple.

Watching, we all held our breath. Clearly we had not had time to school him as to what to do in the event of a Steve sighting.

The unspoken rule was, if you ran into Steve in the hallways, you simply continued on your path. You didn't run up and tell him how much you love the latest iPod or attempt to share a new idea with him. He had his ways of tapping into us to glean the insights he wanted. As much as we all recognized his genius and his growing celebrity, we all knew he would think this behavior was dumb and that we should have more important and meaningful ways to spend our time. I always enjoyed imagining that at some level he was also training us to focus; to zone out the distractions of the world around us, the noise and ever-increasing complexity of our worlds; to concentrate within our own realm on the details, on what was truly important.

Steve was every bit that once-in-a-lifetime human being who warrants endless posthumous imaginings. We all evolved as we watched him evolve, as he shifted the world in accordance with his own shifts of consciousness. My own moments of special exchange with him will remain in my HR chief vault. But as someone who's observed for decades how human beings grow and evolve, I can say he remains, for me, a reason to marvel, far more so than books, movies, or folklore could ever account for.

Dr. Andrew Williams of Spelman College didn't know any of this history. No one had prepped him. Being the kind and unassuming person he was, with his limited knowledge of the CEO of Apple, he walked into this interaction with sincerity and respect. Steve seemed to respond with equal energy; he was gracious, especially once he heard Dr. Williams say, "I am an engineering dean and robotics professor from Spelman College in Atlanta, and we have won several awards. I am very proud of them." We watched Steve engage Dr Williams (and were particularly impressed that he required no history on the significance of Spelman College).

"Really? Do you know how many Black engineers I have right now? None. I need you to help me figure out how to hire Black engineers. Can you spend some time on campus and help us with this?"

We sat amazed. I recalled years earlier when Reverend Jesse Jackson had gotten private audience with Steve to discuss what Rev. Jackson and the Rainbow PUSH Coalition he'd founded called the "digital divide"—the structural and systemic gap between those who were able to benefit from the digital age and those who were not. For years, Congresswoman Barbara Lee and several other members of the Congressional Black Caucus had also been leaning on the tech industry to listen and understand, and to help solve the ever-widening gaps of access and opportunity, disparate resources, and stunning inequities.

I knew Steve was aware of the low representation of women and BIPOC at Apple because of earlier conversations. But I did not expect he'd pitch an outside-the-box idea to a visiting professor from a prominent HBCU, years before the diversity conversation took hold in the mainstream. In retrospect, I should have expected it from him.

And so, in 2005, Dr. Andrew Williams took a sabbatical from Spelman and came to Apple to help recruit Black engineers. He was successful. Not in terms of quantity, but definitely in quality. He hired engineers who made significant contributions and who stayed with Apple long enough to garner impressive career marks. And he took back to Spelman his experiences in the hallowed halls of Cupertino, stories about how Apple employees thought and did things that we were certain no faculty member at Spelman had heard.

And although there has not been a Dr. Williams type scenario since, that experience left a lasting message with all of us involved: that a leader can simply make things happen when they want to, if they are motivated to do so. Period. That was the takeaway. There was no program or precedent, no twenty-five iterations of justification requested. Steve simply acted, and so can any other CEO, leader, or policy maker. Steve did not request benchmarking or the success rates of other programs, because there were none, and he knew it. He innovated in the moment and on a problem he knew required different thinking. This is how power should work: deciding, in the moment, to do things that matter, and not caring about a false sense of viability or optics; simply acting on the rightness of an idea. Being willing to reframe the idea that real shareholder value incorporates socially responsible decisions and deems humanity to be of the greatest value to us all.

Chapter 8

Translators, Interpreters, and Explainers

For you I have written a song,
to be sure that you'll know what I'm saying,
I'll translate as I go along.

—TONY BENNETT,
"FLY ME TO THE MOON"

I was ten when I watched a woman standing on a spotlit platform conduct a master class in communication. I was visiting New York, and my aunt took me to the United Nations, where for a precious few minutes we observed parts of a meeting in the Assembly Hall of the main General Assembly building. From the large mosaic to the chair placement and collection of people, this was, for me, a sacred place where all nations, races, and languages came together in service to the good of the world at large. It wasn't a world leader that captivated me, but an interpreter.

There was something powerful and beautiful in watching this woman listen, internalize, and repeat back what she heard, then offer it to the other side of her dais with grace and nuance. I thought it magnificent and wanted to *be* her. I even noted the physical reaction that occurred when people understood. To facilitate that kind of understanding, the interpreter observed, saw, heard, processed, and used her skills to convey to the receivers. Then she reversed the process. Whoever was at the podium speaking likely had no clue just how much was truly taking place. I didn't fully understand all of what the interpreter did, but I wholeheartedly declared my desire to be one. I saw the magic of a moment when people, races, communities, and nations connected. I wanted to replicate that connection.

Little did I understand then that my presence in so many places as a "first" or an "only," and ultimately my HR career overall, would require me to have a similar skill set, understanding how to interpret and translate the often unspoken and unknown complexities of a corporate ecosystem. At the root, they're two different things: A translator converts text from one language into another, whereas an interpreter translates language, inflection, and meaning back and forth so that it can be understood, often in real time, more broadly by parties from different parts of the world. The resulting connection has the power to shift outcomes that can advance a situation from personal to global. An interpreter must hold words and their power with integrity, with respect.

Today, in many ways interpreting equates to reading a room, then guiding the conversation according to invisible dynamics. I became adept at this early on, able to explain to some people what others were really saying because I understood their history, backstory, and culture.

I'd search my mental files for common human connection points, and because I naturally saw beyond people's protective facades, it was not difficult to weave them into conversation and render uncomfortable moments less so. Interpreting is unlikely to fall squarely into an executive skill matrix, but it certainly found a home in my arc of experiences that focused on people; alongside strategic agility, adaptability, calm composure, and cultural competence—all dimensions of a level of emotional intelligence I did not always realize I had in such abundance.

On a visit to China one September, the senior members of my global teams had gathered. Our agenda was aggressive; we had much to discuss, with decisions to make and to customize for several countries. A big priority was to modify and streamline the existing performance management process to be more straightforward, direct, and globally understood. Some of the clear stars as to why this team was so powerful were present: a British HR executive who'd put together a team that understood the mechanics of every country in Europe, a recruiting team that recognized talent from miles away, and a PhD-level master of leadership who had honed the skills of Apple Store leaders around the world.

Less than two hours into our day, we were knee-deep stuck in language translation challenges. The term "performance management" clearly meant something different in each country, to each leader present.

During these conversations, I noted the change in demeanor of the sole Black man in the room, David, who had significant operations responsibility across geographies. His already quiet demeanor became even more so. I asked him, "David, what are you thinking, something seems suddenly less compelling for you."

He responded without hesitancy, surprising some in the room. "Performance management as we are talking about it, to a Black person is really code for '*We are trying to fire you, but we don't really have a good reason, we just don't see how you fit in, so we will start finding things you are doing wrong, focusing on your attendance, singling you out—it means you are working us out the door.'"*

Facing a room of blank stares, David attempted to explain to the room why he felt this way, and he was immediately countered. Some suggested that this was likely something only he felt, and that he should not feel it, an attempt at righting what felt wrong. A few apologized, as we observed him bristle. Others listened intently, taken aback at this level of outspokenness and energy from their respected colleague. Almost everyone recognized that something important had just happened, something they needed to learn from.

The Japanese team understood it differently as well. In their work culture, the process of managing performance equated to great shame. Of all country teams, they seemed to best understand David's response. At a minimum I believe they related to the layers of lived experiences contained in his words. Whereas the American team continued to speak their own perceptions about David's experiences with well-meaning but microaggressive invalidation, telling him why he was misinterpreting things. I ultimately weighed in to affirm that this was indeed a triggering phrase for many people of color in work situations and had been ages in the making. Our discussion had highlighted the need to align our understanding of performance management, and we eventually did, with new language. Because one individual had spoken out, a critical business process would be better interpreted to more people around the world.

Even with some voices in the room denying David's experience, he had been heard and seen by most. There was enough varied representation present in the room for balance, moving us away from full denial of David's experience and toward considering it weighty enough to make changes. It would be a while before I put it together that I had served as an interpreter of sorts, facilitating a change in differing global views. My ten-year-old dream had come to fruition. We weren't negotiating world peace, but it certainly felt like the stakes for people who struggled with feeling misunderstood and miserable while working were just as high.

The only challenge with what had just transpired was that I was still the only one in that room (as in many others in my experience) seeing the full picture of what was transpiring. I was the natural interpreter. The room was multicultural, but English was still the dominant language, and even with many ethnicities in the room, the English speaking among us expected English understanding, and the Americans centered themselves culturally. The meeting, like so many others, might have moved right along with no recognition that someone had ceased to feel they belonged, pulled away from engaging, paused in consternation over a cultural translation. Perhaps because I knew David, or recognized him culturally, I had sensed he'd left the discussion at some level, and tried to bring him back into it.

The beauty of having more dimensions of humanity represented in more settings is that we are likely to see each other, recognize cultural cues, and be able to act on them, pausing to bring in more clarity and perspective, leaving fewer people behind and psychologically emotionally unaccounted for. The beauty of more dimensions of humans allows for translation of cultural meaning—of inflection, tone, emotional impact—which allows for more people to be a part of the discussion, while we all, even AI, learn something new in the process.

In this example, five people from different countries heard from an American Black man about how his interpretation of "performance management" differed from the English intent, because of his life experiences. And it took a few moments, but his views were ultimately respected and acknowledged, and he was *seen* by his global colleagues.

There were the times when this type of conversation had a different outcome. The Ops team once presented their choice of a bright orange T-shirt color for a Store campaign. It was an aesthetically fun orange, vivid and easily seen from a distance. It took less than five minutes for the two Black and brown people in the room to assert an absolute refusal to ask other Black and brown people across the country to wear the intended shade of orange, all too close to the infamous orange used to identify incarceration. The television hit *Orange Is the New Black* and its double entendre had not yet been created, but the pervasive understanding of the color's implications was quickly understood, and the conversation resolved without debate. We settled on a light teal blue that carried no particular cultural cue.

Sometimes cultural, social, emotional intelligence gets us to better, quickly. Other times it takes years. At any rate or pace, multiple dimensions of people have to be in the rooms where decisions are made, and where technology is created. The work in these rooms is not easier or less, it may even be more intricate, harder at the human level. But it is, again, the real work of building a place of thriving.

In leading people and talent, I often translated the world of Apple for others, especially those new to Silicon Valley culture. That's part of why Apple University was created, specifically to communicate Apple's culture, a key concern Steve held as the company grew. Offerings such as "What Makes Apple, Apple," the storied course in high demand across the company, or "Gould's Variation"—a course taught by a celebrated Stanford professor on Toronto pianist Glenn Gould's meticulous attention to detail—were effective and popular, yet for many employees without access to Apple University courses, where would they go for interpretation? Where were they going to fill these critical cultural gaps? How were they even supposed to know who or what to ask? Most of them managed to glean insight via networking, both formally and informally, finding the answers they needed to navigate their day to day. Some made miscalculations. Some reached out to me, others to HR, others to sources outside of Apple, in whatever ways they could muster, to help crack codes, search for context, or read between lines. The level of effort expended was unfortunate, yet the amount of resilience they developed was commendable. They were smart, curious people, and they figured things out. It was fascinating to watch them develop and apply problem-solving skills, but disappointing to observe the necessity for their effort.

Many well-meaning managers tried to close context gaps for how to understand Apple. The challenge was these managers themselves did not always recognize the gaps, they simply never had to. Those who needed the insight represented very small numbers within tech communities. That meant, within tech culture, that we, our visibility or lack thereof, just did not register on the "oh I get it now" meter for even the most grounded and astute managers. The dearth of sight was and is still significant. Very few leaders understood this, and although clearly not unique to Apple, invisibility as a BIPOC theme is still so common that it is still discussed in seminars, social gatherings, professional organizations, DEI meetings, blogs to barber shops, and in general, deemed a part of the "Working While Black" experience.

When the first class from the Thurgood Marshall College Fund (TMCF) program arrived on campus, we attempted to fill in some of those gaps. My team and I became my early life memory version of a United Nations interpreter team for this predominantly Black intern class who found themselves at a Silicon Valley technology company, some thousands of miles from home, in a land never before visited.

As an HBCU graduate, I understood what this experience might feel like for many of the students. From my experience in talent management, I also understood the untapped ecosystem of the STEM talent in the HBCU communities, even if many of my colleagues considered an HBCU education "subpar" compared to students from PWIs (predominantly white institutions)—long a persistent, broadly held bias.

The origin and the need for the creation of America's Historically Black Colleges and Universities was born out of post–Civil War social and racial inequality. And as time passed, not much changed for hopes of education for Black Americans. Put simply, Black colleges survived for years under disparate funding practices, with no funding for technology, labs, research, infrastructure, and scarce opportunities for exposure to corporations with fast-paced, forward-facing enterprise and consumer technology. That Black colleges boasted thousands of innovative, creative students, young people, and dedicated faculty who managed to thrive under these long disparate conditions speaks to their creativity and resilience.

I'd understood for decades how HBCUs were disproportionately resourced, making do with an embarrassing fraction of what other institutions received from state governments, donors, foundations, and alumni. I recall driving the rural road to Grambling past the idyllic Louisiana Tech University in Ruston, Louisiana, and shaking my head at the stark differences in the campuses. The state of Louisiana poured tons of money into Louisiana Tech while ignoring its neighbor, Grambling; a well-documented pattern repeated in state university systems in North Carolina, Texas, Arkansas, Florida, Alabama, and more. (In September of 2023, the Departments of Education and Agriculture sent letters to sixteen governors of states with Land Grant HBCUs, calculating the disparity in funding to be up to $12 billion, just from 1987 to 2020. The departments asserted that states opening land grant universities serving Black students were required to provide an equitable distribution of state funds to institutions founded between 1862 and 1890. Only two states, Delaware and Ohio, have complied with this law.)

Because I had this context, I believed Apple could do something significant within the HBCU communities and make an important statement of leadership. I set up meetings with the leadership of TMCF. Its namesake, U.S. Supreme Court Justice Thurgood Marshall, the first Black Supreme Court justice, had specifically fought for the rights of Black Americans to be educated in the era of separate but equal, which resulted in the landmark *Brown v. Board of Education* case. I was particularly interested in this organization, as there were fifteen Black engineering schools in membership with TMCF. In addition to the engineering deans of these schools, TMCF had successfully partnered with major corporate industry leaders for internship programs committing to longer-term relationships, rather than the standard model of a short summer interning stint. As a result, TMCF was seeing promising outcomes for long-term career opportunities for their students. I wanted that for Apple too.

When I met the leadership team at TMCF, it was an eye-to-eye, heart-to-heart connection. Their team sat alongside mine and fully understood each other across the table, but even more, resonated with each team's vision and desire to go deeper and further. In my mind, the real purpose of this partnership with TMCF had always been to *mutually* educate, to identify and mitigate biases, and to ensure that students received greater benefis than the nice letter of completion and a high hope of subsequent job offers. The TMCF president Johnny Taylor and I could not have been more in sync on how we saw the partnership, and what we wanted it to achieve. We recognized the quick backlash to the announcement of the partnership and the critics lobbing doubts in our direction. We both knew there were long-standing barriers to our vision, and yet set out to change them.

For example, there was the idea that HBCUs derived some benefit from the good optics of having our best and brightest "compete" with white students from top white schools. In other words, a reinforcing of the subtle message that HBCU students were less desirable. This was nonsense; HBCUs wanted fundamental access to opportunities, not good optics. Then there was the belief that HBCU students must demonstrate their worthiness to be employed by the companies they sought to work for. This was more reinforcing of the age-old "work harder because you are less capable" trope.

The belief was held that corporations could offer intern programs at minimal cost, followed by lower-level job offers, and still secure the goodwill of the community. This may have been true in the past, but through representation within companies, consumerism, and general marketplace savvy, the Black community at large became more informed about the internal structures, opportunities, and inequities within companies, and more vocal about this knowledge.

Last, we had to combat the broadly held perception that HBCUs are substandard, and in some instances statistics were used as a matter of "proof." Yet, no stats were known or offered on the legacy of inequality these schools faced down for generations, their resilience or longevity, and how they managed to remain so little known as they continued, against all odds, to produce excellence. Companies should have been swarming onto HBCU campuses studying the culture and techniques that have built and sustained the levels of resilience and achievement we've come to know.

Whenever I could, I challenged the unspoken (and sometimes spoken) HBCU misperceptions. Yes, there were definite truths about the state of many HBCUs. There were stark realities the Black community understood and accepted about the history of the schools' existence. But I was on a mission to enlighten those assigning blame solely upon the schools, faculty, staff, and even the students themselves, instead of the historical systems that created and perpetuated their legacy of struggle. Most important, we needed to separate the students from this line of blaming, as it meant they again carried far too much "burden of proof" of their value.

In the corporate world overall, and especially in tech, the concept of internships as "diversity outreach" into any underserved community still remains fraught with "one way-isms." While they are provided meager budgets they barely miss, few companies make any attempt at mutual learning, do any diligence on outcomes, any work to shift biases, or attempt to address real challenges. Few companies invest the time to track their interns, get to know them, and understand how best to retain them and ensure their success. And if an outstanding intern program does capture this insight, it is dismissed by the time it reaches hiring decision-makers.

One HR chief from a well-known company shared with me that her hiring managers were annoyed about having to implement a "diversity" intern program; they insisted that the HBCU students be treated "exactly the same" as the PWI students. Claiming to be concerned about possible accusations of unfairness, they backed away from any hint of an attempt to offer HBCU students equal advantages and access. Backlash had taken its usual place, right on the heels of any real movement toward equity.

And what could have possibly been more unfair than the reality of why the country needed HBCUs to begin with? According to Thurgood Marshall College Fund's program managers, many of the larger corporate participants in various industries were making headway with their participation and engagement, creating meaningful career tracks and longer-term relationships for returning students—but tech companies were either engaging very minimally or not participating at all.

The tech industry's biased perceptions about engineering and STEM talent ran deep, and was not limited to HBCU perceptions. Graduates of nondistinctive state colleges, community colleges, vocational schools, all suffered under tech recruiting lenses. Matching technology vision with technology elite schools was nothing unusual, just increasingly impractical and did not adequately serve economic growth for companies. As several tech companies became more fully realized big businesses, able to offer broad job opportunities for many other degree tracks in finance, business, operations, law, and marketing, they were not taking advantage of this talent position. These openings weren't being promoted into Black and brown talent communities, or even more mainstream pools across the country. And the rarely challenged perceptions or myths of what schools were most effective were allowed to become blind spots, limiting opportunities for students and for companies. Generally, tech companies moved too fast and furious to even know they were missing talent opportunities or to care that their blind spots were costing them cultural sight impairment.

I had a deep understanding of the Black college campus and what it took for many of the students to make the leap of faith and land at a tech company in California. In the design phase of the TMCF program, we knew it would be generally expected that the students (or any BIPOC hires) would "adjust"—they'd adapt themselves to the environments and subcultures they found themselves assigned to. If they did not adapt, the problem was theirs because of their less-than-standard educational experience from a "Black college." Or worse, because they themselves were somehow less capable, slower to learn.

These perceptions were rarely overtly stated but were loudly practiced at nearly every tech company, as their Black staff would share. I knew that for these students, coming from HBCU campuses, traveling west and reporting in to work in

Cupertino, California, or anywhere in the Valley was no easy adjustment. I'd had my own emerging experience from an HBCU years ago, and I understood how enormous the belonging gap could be for an HBCU student entering corporate culture for the first time.

I knew the students would be highly tech savvy, but they might not be tech *culture* savvy. Meaning not that they were incapable of learning, but that they needed access, exposure, immersion, time, coaching, and support. And they needed it because socially constructed inequities existed as barriers to it. They did not need it because they were less capable. But for years of my career life both personally and in talent roles for companies, I'd spend time closing this gap, via translating, interpreting, code-switching, and educating. Modifications I believe are easily made through process and education. As futile as it seemed then, I didn't give up and I'm fairly certain if faced with the very same exhausting narratives, I would not give up today; just likely with far less patience for institutional privilege and with my always graceful reserve saved for something more worthy. By now we should be better. By now most of us who do this work know, when the Equity in the DEI investment formula is presented to a company's leadership, they raise a typical plethora of objections. The pushback—what we who do this work know as backlash—is irrational and predictable. "There are not enough resources or time," leaders say; it's "not fair" and we must be "fair to all" and in so doing, dismiss the difficult legacy of how we got here. With PWI students or potential hires ready and able to plug right into these roles today, why extend these resources? Why address the discomfort this approach causes? Ah . . . because that is the real work of DEI. Facing down the discomfort of the *why*.

The first cohort of TMCF students were brilliant, savvy, and ready for the challenge. But perhaps less ready for the culture shock of stepping into a less-than-warm, confusing, white corporate world. I could see and feel their apprehension, the defense gymnastics going on inside for them as they entered Apple's campus buildings. I understood that their adjustment meant establishing cultural infrastructure; finding a Black barber, hair braider, church, soul food spot, social gathering place in Cupertino or the neighboring Bay Area communities. It meant drives to Oakland, Emeryville, Alameda, and a calculation of the time and energy required to sustain a newly created lifestyle framework.

I heard students say, "I never in a million years imagined I would be somewhere like Apple." And why shouldn't they have imagined that? As weeks passed, it was joyful to observe students' shifting perception of being a part of Apple, whether during "pinch me" moments of receiving an offer to work on Siri, on some unnamed confidential Apple project, or having a chat with former Vice President Al Gore as he headed to the fourth floor for a board meeting. I saw anxiety give way to relief when on a Friday afternoon the interns realized they were included on the invite list for an iconic Silicon Valley beer bash, with hundreds of employees in the campus atrium and Pharrell Williams performing.

For an HBCU intern's first turn in a technology company thousands of miles from home, I was their frequent interpreter—and they had questions.

"Why is it okay to just show up at your professional job with some raggedy shorts on, a crumpled T-shirt, and questionable hygiene? This is not what I was taught, but here it seems like the norm," said one young woman, rather taken aback by the implication that appearance was inconsequential.

"Do people here just not even look up to acknowledge other people when they talk to you? I don't even know if they are talking to me or if they even know I am standing there. I don't know if I can ask any questions," said an intern from a southern Black community where this scenario would be considered profoundly disrespectful.

Had I been simply translating the "come and be as you are" culture of Silicon Valley, I would have just explained that the culture tries to be conducive to focusing on work, and that being comfortable and casual enhances focus, so minimal attention to appearance was necessary. But I chose to say more, to interpret more thoroughly, because I understood the context of the intern's background. I was happy to explain: "Dressing that casually, interacting that aloofly, is probably not a strategy that works the same for everyone. For us it's important to feel good about our professional presence, and how *we* show up, because we know that historically we have always felt we were our better selves when we looked our best. Feeling great about our collective presentation is ours culturally to own. You don't have to conform or dress down." I was interpreting between tech culture and historical tradition, incorporating what was psychologically important for people so new to the tech world, earnest in their desire to fit in, to be seen, to be understood.

I wish there had been many more interpreters, able to see, hear, and recognize the students, who they were, their concerns and desires. I wish there had been more folks like me in various tech companies, interpreting the HBCU legacy and success formula to key decision-makers. Far more Damien Hooper-Campbells or Fred Humphries at Microsoft who'd collaborated with me on getting an HBCU student hired between our two companies.

And I believed that through a well-designed immersion experience, partnered with good, solidly empathetic managers and mentors, the students would flourish and much of their reticence would dissolve, replaced by enthusiasm and focus. But far more important for me was what the Apple community could be learning from the students.

One Apple leader absolutely understood. A former Stanford professor, he traveled with my team to Jackson, Mississippi, to Jackson State University, and met their engineering school dean. A renowned scholar himself, my colleague came away from the trip sharing that he'd seen and experienced a day of historical significance unlike any he'd ever known. That alone said to me that with intentional design and proper support, this could be a program that shifted consciousness. It supported my belief that much of what is required for significant movement in "diversity" is a mutual value exchange and greater understanding of the "why." It reinforced my long-standing hope of companies seeing that through this lens of mutuality *the company itself* would enjoy real gains, valuable truths, cultural perspective, and historical insights that could help them crack the code of representation.

Yet we still are not having these qualitative conversations about programs or honest discussions about diverse hiring.

The quiet part no one wants to admit is that when a person of color is hired and enters a work environment, there are still those same questions: about their abilities, their background, their day-to-day demonstrations. They are quietly still auditioning for the roles they've already been hired for, possibly for years after, constantly needing to prove they deserve to be where they are. They are judged more frequently, longer, and through more challenging lenses than their white and non-Black counterparts. This quiet and often subconscious hazing that people of color are subjected to equates, sadly, to a longer journey to belonging, if it is ever reached at all. This is still where we are, and I'm not sure I can name a single person of a BIPOC group who has not experienced this.

How does this change? It changes when instead of knee-jerk denial there is honest, uncomfortable acknowledgment that this is still happening. It changes when there is willingness to want to know *why* this is happening. It changes when there is a willingness to rethink the systems that have maintained the status quo that allows this to still happen.

Things can change when missteps occur and mistakes are made. Consumers respect accountability and subsequent learning admissions from company leaders. For people who take leading seriously, the idea of growing and maturing from change this significant is actually appealing. Things change when we allow smart, emotionally intelligent, resilient leaders to lead in their own unique ways, without fear of reprimand or retaliation. Things change when top executives behave inspirationally, not punitively. Huge shifts happen culturally when mistakes are seen as a way of learning and innovating, and when saying "I don't know" is not an indicator of weakness. And there is decidedly change when leaders have the courage to stave off pressure to overdeliver on results with a surefooted assurance that people are being considered, seen, and their value understood.

I've witnessed each of these stated examples, and the associated shifts. The examples I've witnessed demonstrated authentic empathetic leadership, and evolution into a more emotionally intelligent organization. Yet we still are not quickly, readily choosing this path. But when we do, the human spirit moves within the organization, and it is a power lever that works. It is the human spirit that truly carries a business to its highest success.

Chapter 9

Please Allow Me to Express Myself

I'm the best, 'cause God said so.
I'm just trying to express my lyrical flow.

—TALIB KWELI, "OH MY STARS"

In my early working years, I was frequently told I had "potential." I was never quite certain what I had potential for based on the vagueness of these assertions, but I wanted to believe that meant something positive, albeit never tangible. I was often placed on "high potential" lists. This also was intended to translate to me as positive, an indication of favor, of being endorsed, so to speak. Hopeful of a path toward expanding my influence, these seemed like the right conversations to be having—until it became apparent that my male colleagues appeared to be skipping the "potential" step and moving straight to "promotable" and even "promoted." Somehow extra steps had been added to my progression when I wasn't watching . . . and with no explanation as to why, except for the frequent use of the word "readiness." When it became apparent that I was already "ready," well-prepared, and in most instances exceeded the readiness, preparation, and performance of my already-getting-promoted white-guy counterparts, I ceased to place value in this terminology, dropping it into my code-translation glossary, fiftieth edition, and by now a reference I used frequently as an intervention to help others when they hit these same barriers.

We want to believe that if we are in or a part of a place, we have the same chances for acceptance, approval, and support for belonging as anyone. But, if we fall outside of the dominant profile in some way, our path seems to suddenly meander or is blocked altogether. The pace changes, criteria shift. In my early working years there seemingly existed some other assessment manual for women and for "others." This alternate assessment manual was both clandestine yet close by and convenient for its users. I never saw it physically, yet I could spot it a block away as it made its way into conversations with my managers, suddenly shifting the mental focus from the content of the discussion to exasperating "What just happened?" or "What did he just say?" moments. Often, as the communities of people who know this pattern find one another, we'd gather to affirm the oddness of this behavior and frequently story swap about our experiences.

Despite recognizing the signs, I certainly asked what constituted "promotable" for me versus others. My inquiries were often met with pauses followed by interesting assertions, such as: I was more people-oriented than business-oriented, an advocate for individuals more so than for management. But wasn't *that* my job? Why did they not see that having someone employees believed they could trust was a strategic business asset?

Once I opened the feedback door, my managers would rush through it, relishing the opportunity to tell me how to get where they were. I was told I was "really smart, but too soft-spoken," as male colleagues talked over and interrupted me.

There was also "super knowledgeable but too nice" whenever I opted to look at ways to value people, save jobs, or salvage dignity. What was saved in time, expenses, or litigation somehow did not connect directly to having treated people with compassion and respect, but instead these traits were viewed as "nice," and therefore dismissed. If a discussion led with context and backstory, ensuring a full picture of the potential impact on people, I'd be quickly prompted to "get to the numbers," even though ultimately it would be the human conversations that presented the most challenge, supported or disproved the "numbers," and required the most delicate handling.

I was often encouraged to "cut to the chase" of human dilemmas, meaning that taking time for anything but a manager's account of a situation was too time-consuming. The details managers did not want to be troubled with ultimately were the details they had to be troubled with, the challenges they had to navigate. And in situations involving people least like their profile, people they needed to better understand, learn from and see, these situations ofttimes became tutorial. They'd all too often include post-training or coaching that forced late lessons we could have learned earlier. My adjustment to this reality meant learning to start every discussion and conversation in a very agentic way, the ways in which my dominant profile colleagues insisted upon, the ways that kept them comfortable enough to listen and to hear me out. Once an issue was laid out, I could slowly present optional ways of seeing the problem to a solution, options that incorporated room for people to feel heard. People feeling heard is often all that is needed to dissipate, diffuse, and even course correct. In my mind I could hear my mother saying "I just needed to speak my peace to it," as she moved intricately through life.

My early working years of manager feedback resulted in equal amounts confusion, with the realization that I was surrounded by humans lacking in human skill. I, in turn, spent too much time and life essence trying to convince them of my value, abundant in human skill. I don't recall exactly the point in time I gave up trying, deciding instead to just "do my job" and not try to convince anyone that we could fare so much better if we did better by people.

I hoped at some point people would just get it (and "get" me!). Looking back, it wasn't possible for me to just "do a job," as it meant becoming transactional and soulless. I knew I was not a quiet placeholder, but a powerful knower and seer, awaiting my time to apply what I did naturally and with great benefit to the enterprise. I had no idea at the time that my opportunity would eventually be an entire global reality of technology stores, but I was convinced it would reveal itself. And with some help and wisdom from people who *did* see me, I settled into what it felt like to be emotionally intelligent and almost always many steps ahead of my colleagues, always having to bring them along or wait for them to catch up. And although I allowed those years of having that dimension of my talent suppressed to weigh too heavily upon my psyche, I believed the human visionaries who predicted that EQ (emotional intelligence), empathy, and human-centered thinking would become desirable, even in demand. Often frustrated, I knew I was showing up as less of who I was, yet I still held hope for a broader realization that being fundamentally human-centered was the smarter and most expeditious way to do business of any kind, and that to do so equated to more of all kinds of people being centered, included, and having a fair and decent shot at eventually thriving.

. . .

During my time in Silicon Valley, I recall walking a team of startup leaders through the Jungian-based DiSC assessment with an outside consultant and an industrial psychologist. DiSC, which stands for (D)ominance, (i)nfluence, (S)teadiness, and (C)onscientiousness, is broadly considered to be a universal behavioral model, admittedly created in an era of even less diversity, yet supposedly purely personality based. We intended to use the results to help us sort out the best leadership roles for each member as we approached a critical round of funding. I was the only person of any color, with one other woman executive and five white men, two of them the company founders, one European, one Canadian, and one highly introverted.

I scored highest in the group in influence (i) and lower in dominance (D). Three of my colleagues—the other woman, the introvert, and the Canadian—recommended that I take the lead on several topics for the pitch meeting with Goldman Sachs. These three also did not fit the desired mold of leading with dominance, but they pushed hard for my influence leanings. The founders overruled their choice, saying I would not be aggressive enough in my approach. My towering score in influence was ignored.

I was disappointed. I spent the next few weeks or even months trying to appear more "dominant." I asked for feedback from various "dominant" team members on how to beef up my ability to "debate" (interrupt and argue), undervaluing my own strong ability to influence, because when it came to decisions, damn my influence, the dominant folks simply dominated. Looking back, it was all somewhat ironic, humorous, and great potential fodder for *The Office* episodes, except that, sadly, it was a waste of my energy. Unbeknownst to me until much later, it was also stressful for others observing me and how I was being treated. Managers take note: People are always watching and watching how those "first and only" are able to thrive as an indication of their chances of doing so.

Within organizations, "others" (not male nor white) are encouraged, coached, and performance managed to fashion ourselves to conform to an unachievable profile, when the reality is that we represent a world of new insight and perspectives. In imagining a world where "we" have a shorter journey to belonging, where "we" are offered feedback that takes advantage of the gifts we bring with us instead of insisting they be left behind, I can envision a kind of thriving that for years I longed to experience.

In the earliest years of my career, what I called "comfort policies" were put in place by companies, residue from the 1980s, echoing an industrial era when the human objective was to maintain the comfort of the few by sacrificing the comfort of the many. These policies avoided messy or uncomfortable conversations and disciplined anyone initiating them. Politics, religion, and race were touchy areas to be avoided lest an issue be raised to HR, who would then point to the "comfort policies" and require containment.

Of course, the "comfort zone" was, by default, what was comfortable for white and male dominated rooms. For women, discussions about family, children (athletic excellence excepted), health, pregnancy, even career were deemed outside of the comfortable-for-guys zone. If you were Black, talking about any aspect of Black experience needed to be done jokingly or include an accepted category such as sports or entertainment (with the exception of February Black History Month conversations). Any race-related discussion raised the uncomfortable-for-white-people meter, leading to awkward silences, sidelong glances, downcast eyes, and ultimately abrupt topic changes laced with nervous sighs of relief.

So despite the posted commitments to the contrary, for at least a decade of my earliest work life, the full breadth of my identity was quietly instructed to be left at home. Social matters were discouraged from any discussion. Expecting the dominant culture to take note of my Blackness and femaleness was an unnecessary inconvenience. It simply did not matter to them, a fact they thought was redeeming. Cultural awareness was nonexistent. My stomach tightened when a white person attempted to speak on a matter about which they were quite unenlightened. If a woman dared to assert a point of view on gender equity or representation of women, the men in charge of all things raced to change the topic. "Let's take that offline" was a preferred shutdown.

So it is no wonder that the shift into an era where people may suddenly bring their full stories to bear—and with them their political and philosophical opinions, beliefs, and stances—has forced corporate culture-keepers to confront the human emotions and design challenges this shift ushers into working places. Where do we fit in all this humanity? How do we make it all coexist and not impede the mission of the organization, inconvenience our timelines, diminish our comfort? How do we, in a seismically shifted world, make things go back to "sorta like they were"? We don't. We have to relearn human interaction and reimagine what it might be like to thrive in it.

Today, we do appear to be making an orchestrated effort to

bring humanness into business, but in stages we can see, understand, and digest. Being human does make business sense. Environments where people behave authentically and empathetically will make some uncomfortable. Some of that discomfort will be more complicated by representation; by experiences of people never heard, let alone seen and centered. More BIPOC coming into organizations will demand space to exist, and in doing so will shapeshift the business world as we know it.

A decade or so ago, the comedy duo Key and Peele were masters of illustrating code-switching to hilarious ends: from Luther, President Obama's anger translating alter ego, to the clip, also of President Obama, greeting dignitaries with decidedly different gestures. What makes Jordan Peele's portrayal so incredibly funny is its absolute truth; it did happen and at the highest echelon of social order, as we recall President Obama's more formal handshake with a white coach in contrast to his full-body greeting of NBA player Kevin Durant. It was, to us, a perfect example, and moreover, a demonstration of the fact that even a POTUS was not exempt from the need, or the desire, to code-switch. It was a cultural transition he naturally made—and chose to make.

Historically, code-switching was a survival skill for enslaved African people. I would argue that it still is. The Obama examples highlighted when it has been our choice, infusing it with proper grace and flair, and the Key and Peele bits allow us to see the act with humor and appreciation of its facility in our lives and culture. My favorite moment of having a complete miss in my translation skills was on a visit to Capitol Hill where a small group of colleagues and I were given audience by then Congressman and head of the Congressional Black Caucus, the very esteemed G. K. Butterfield. Having little knowledge of who I sat in front of, I proceeded to share the PR-prepared, bullet point narrative of progress we were making in tech, or attempting to make. How did I manage to miss that my words were not landing with the Congressman and likely annoying as hell? I ended my little spiel and he paused—that southern kind of pause when you suddenly realize you just may have entered a zone you are *not* prepared for. "Are you quite finished, Miss Young Smith? Thank you for your remarks, now let me make you aware of how far off the mark Silicon Valley is to the reality of our communities." And there we sat in silence, listening, absorbing what really mattered, and how never to waste the time of someone whose life's work was dedicated to equality and freedom, struggle, and hard-fought victories. You listened, you learned, you asked what you could and should do. Period. No translation. No switching of code. Direct, clear, precise. I took this lesson into the presence of other leaders I was privileged to meet; Representatives Emanuel Cleaver, Barbara Lee, Maxine Waters, and the late Congressman John Lewis. No translation required.

I think of effective code-switching like a smoothly executed vocal passaggio, moving up or down vocal registers with no discernible transition. I began to code-switch long before learning that there was a name for it, that it was a *thing*, and that it began centuries ago. Linguists first named this learned skill in the 1950s as the forced ability to switch identities or speak differently to survive physically, economically, and psychologically. But writers from earlier eras detailed it without naming it. In Jean Toomer's novel, *Cane,* published in 1923, the characters, like most Black Americans today, inhabit two worlds: the public, around whites and non-Blacks, and the private, among loved ones, friends, and community.

I was the kid who "spoke well," which in the 1970s meant I spoke with what the elders of my childhood called "perfect diction": no discernible accent, no regional dialect, and no lapse in grammatical standards. I spoke softly, but directly, and correctly as per Oxford and Merriam-Webster, which, by the way, without siblings around, I'd study in my room as a kid.

In elementary school, my classmates called me "smart," which I relished. I was also told, "You talk like a white girl," which I did not relish, as it seemed a sort of condemnation of something that felt very natural and insignificant to me. I just *spoke*—without effort or affectation.

"You speak exactly the way you speak, and you do not change it. You are smart, and you speak in a way that will get you respect!" asserted my Brooklyn-raised mother. My Louisiana-born father more reflectively said, "Don't ever let anyone talk you out of who you are."

I absorbed their advice but silently committed to knowing how to speak to whom, when, and why. That was the beginning of my ability to be multilingual; to know how to switch and when, and how to be interpretive or translative, as situations required. My first impulse to consciously code-switch was when Darlita Cross, a fiery girl in my fifth grade, picked a fight with me for answering too many questions in class.

Darlita looked like me but believed that I thought I was "better than everyone else" because I was constantly raising my hand in class. I suppose Darlita had enough of my question-answering, because one day she looked at me and said icily, "Meet me after school, I'mma show you."

At that moment, I felt like the blood left my body, and possibly the air too. What did I do to her?

The next day I and my small gaggle of friends, all mildly terrified about what to expect, met Darlita on the playground. She started screaming, "You're a showoff, a smarty pants, and I'm gonna teach you a lesson, missy." I tried to reason with her, but I'd already learned from life experience that there's no reasoning with an angry person.

Darlita came at me, pushing me, and I was too horrified that this was even happening to call upon any of the pillow-punching skills my dad had taught me! I thought I was toast until Ricky Lewis, a rough-and-tumble older kid, came over, handed me a tire iron, and told me to "use this." Of course, I did not, but just held it frozen in my hands, and suddenly the fight was over. I didn't know what had happened, only that someone unexpected had shown up for me and summarily ended the fight.

Darlita walked away laughing, while I walked home shaken and upset. *How did this happen? How should I be tomorrow? Should I not raise my hand in class anymore? Should I try to speak in a different way? Will we fight every day now?* But just as suddenly, in a plot twist I did not see coming, Darlita became my newest friend. She said, "Yeah, so what, you're smart, I'm not mad about it any-more." A playground teacher questioned us both about the incident, but neither of us said anything, both adhering to an unspoken agreement: we would not admit that two Black girls had fought, as we'd both suffer the consequences.

This is now one of the fondest (and funniest) memories of my childhood, and I think in some way it was a call to action: If I was going to speak the way I did, and show up the way I did, I needed to also remember where I came from—my people, my community. So from that day forward I became fluent in both languages. Darlita made me realize that I had to navigate this world with my own cultural language as core. That everywhere I went, I might need to be able to switch, but that I would always have a home language: words and phrases I used when I needed to relate, to feel safe and seen. And that because I was "smart," I'd develop the ability to switch early and to always know when things were safe, when I was safe. She made sure I understood this, and I hope wherever she is, she knows I am grateful.

It took me longer to figure out that code-switching isn't just about how we speak—it's also about how we look. For Black women, hair is existential and informs how we show up in this life. It is also deeply cultural. We are inspired by it, shaped by it, live and die by it. We express the entire narratives of our lives through our hair. Our babies' hair is studied and cultivated, to determine the personality of its texture and how it will be cared for. Last burial wishes might include how our hair will look at a final viewing and through eternal rest. The emotional attachment we have to hair will never be fully understood by anyone other than Black women. It is sacred. It is art. It is us.

The fact that a law had to be passed to eliminate discrimination over Black women's hair underscores just how fraught the hair issue became for Black women. The first CROWN Act (which stands for Create a Respectful and Open World for Natural Hair)—a law which prohibits discrimination based on hair style and hair texture—was adopted in California in July 2019. Since then, similar statutes have been passed by twenty states and thirty cities. Needing a law to protect our right to simply *be* is beyond comprehension. This battle over hair seemed to be born of misunderstanding, resentment, suppression, and willful obstinance. And it has been a breathtaking waste of time. We will always show up with hair consciousness. We will always manage to live in this impossible place of having to defend our authentic genetic manifestation, all the while still expressing ourselves proudly, regally, invincibly.

I don't remember when I first laid eyes on my dad's Louisiana cousins, but I remember being transfixed. They were beautiful women, with southern femininity laced with a "don't try me" attitude. They shared a lilt in their speech, a spraying of beautiful freckles, confidence, swerve, and shades of golden, red, and honey-colored hair. Their complexions varied as well: Edith was honey colored, Vera Mae and Lela Mae were bronze and cocoa hued, and when they moved, the golden hair followed. I was mesmerized, not just by their red-headedness and golden blond glow, but by their sheer regality. They were royal from my vantage point, and from that moment forward, I held honey golden–hued hair as an icon of Black beauty.

My personal style has always been expressive; my mother,

aunts, and those gorgeous cousins were my models. I inherited the idea that our clothes and hair are an important form of expression, and we would not think of going out into the world without giving thought and care to that expression. "How are you wearing your hair?" was less a concern of style and more a question of "How do you need to feel?" It was not for others; it was for us.

In my early years of work life, I changed my hair all the time, and it never failed to garner the attention of coworkers.

"You changed your hair!" someone would announce on my behalf as I walked into a meeting. As if I was not aware of this fact, and also as if I had not sat for a few well-spent hours to enact this change. But few in the room knew the realities of a Black hair salon.

"How long did that take?"

"Two hours," I fibbed. It was more like four or more for braiding, and my natural locs required even longer for meticulous individual grooming.

"Does it hurt?"

"No." (Seriously, do you have nerve endings in *your* hair?)

"It makes you look so different!"

"That is kind of the point." (Internal eye roll.)

"Can you wash it?"

"Yes. Daily, just as you do." (Seriously, are you now questioning my hygiene?)

"Wow, my hair would never do that!" (Of course it won't; your hair doesn't do what mine does.)

This. Was. Constant. I would change my hair, have it called out in open discussion, and interrogation ensued.

Straighten my hair? Same thing, but with a twist.

"Wow, your hair looks great, I really like this style the best!"

"I wonder why that is." (Of course you like it the way you are most comfortable with . . . straight, like yours.)

"It's so long!" (Yes, surprise, my hair is curly but long, and can be both.)

"What do you have to do to get it so straight?" (Be handy with a blow-dryer and curling iron. Not rocket science.)

"Wow, that is so much trouble . . I could never take that much time every morning!" (Because hair is meaningless to you. And you are not me.)

And so it went. I continued to change my hair in accordance with my mood, over the years shifting style, color, extensions, wraps, blunt cuts, flat ironed, twists, locs, and the questions came as rapid as my changes. I answered them and, when I felt like it, tossed in a truth, a truth, and a fib to amuse myself and to allay the sheer cringe of it all. It was part of being from a culture where hair was expressive and working in places where it was not, and being summarily misunderstood by society at large.

Often, I made bets with myself on who'd comment, what questions would be asked, and how quickly we'd have my hair discussion before shifting to the business at hand. It was a game, and most Black women in corporate America are reluctantly good players.

What was not a game was the aggregated effect of the microaggressions woven into these kinds of questions: the hints of judgment and xenophobia, and the opting out of any responsibility to try understanding outside of one's own familiarity. It was simply okay to question, stare, and offer commentary. My "state of hair" was always on display and up for debate. A simple "Denise has changed her hair again" might have been okay if not accompanied by the idea that it was both novel and frivolous, for vanity, style, or even attention. Insinuations that were both annoying and false.

What was also not a game was me believing I had to accept that this would always happen and I'd have to brace myself for the unwanted attention. What is not a game is how routinely this conversation repeats in every work setting where Black women exist. It is indicative of the utter disinterest in developing cultural competence by those who believe their centering to be the standard, the norm.

· · ·

Now and then, I took a risk to pull the curtains back on my own code-switching, sharing with a few coworkers what it was like to try to sustain these dual aspects of life. How it felt to balance the human desire to be seen, to speak multiple work languages, to stave off microaggressions *Matrix*-like, to be my best self, to advocate for those without a voice, and still be a contributing professional.

I shared that we were encouraged to emulate them if we hoped to progress our own livelihoods, and not because we aspired to be them but because we had to exist in an environment where they could not experience discomfort; because when they were uncomfortable, it meant we were not safe. I related experiences they were familiar with. I spoke with genuine compassion, knowing what I was saying would be new for them and hard for them to absorb. And as much as I amusedly wished for my own version of Luther, the anger translator Key and Peele created for their fictional Obama, I had developed my own internal translation app for their responses.

A coworker might say, "You don't need to do any of this. Why in the world would you need to carry all of this? It's just not necessary!" Translation: We don't feel it, so you should not, and if you do, we are telling you that you don't have to, as it is our version of your world that should prevail.

Or how about, "I never knew this was happening, why has no one else raised this?" Translation: This has to be your own personal issue, because no one else has validated what you are telling me.

Or, "You are overreacting. If we talk over you, just speak up louder. Everyone has to fight to be heard! That's our culture. It's competitive! We have great team energy! Just go with the flow." Translation: Our competitive male behavior is the desired and dominant culture; we have no need for change, and you are the outlier. Fix you, not us.

Fine, the people constituting "others" would say. We are accustomed to this, to you being centered. We have years of expertise succeeding even though our starting point is always somewhere subterranean. Even though we are required to study and know everything possible about you ... data and metadata. Yet about us you remain uninformed, unaware, and flatly ignorant. Explaining things from this baseline is tiring, yet we continue trying because we also know you are essentially cheating yourselves out of our full brilliance. And it means that for each day of living with the additional emotional taxation of being othered we lose, but so do you. We hurt, and you do as well, even unknowingly. For every instance, remark, situation, incident that feels like a toxic dart hit us, we, the othered, woman-up; like the action movie hero shot down, but not down enough to die. That is how microaggression feels to me physically. The dart depletes a full measure of strength, and as the dart shooter stands oblivious to the harm done, the shot lingers with dull stinging. The accumulated effect eventually proves fatal.

We then respond, maybe thoughtfully, but with well-practiced form, deciding in that moment which response is worth our time. Often I made the conscious decision to say nothing, to stay safe from an emotionally and culturally careless, trauma-causing manager. Safe from harm, so says the song.

But what else sits in that quiet? For women, Black people, people of color, it is the reality of constantly assessing how safe we are, how understood, believed, valued, how *seen*. When we are quiet, when those with power are speaking at us, around us, but not with us, who is making decisions about our well-being? When we feel the need to be so guardedly silent, who then can try to know us, really?

But it doesn't end there. If we do say something, will the one conversation when we speak out be the one that is jeopardizing our job? The one that suddenly causes me to be considered a "concern"? Should anyone having an othering experience risk raising it to an untrained and equally-culturally-bereft HR department? To someone designated to "solve the problem," which is us, then requiring we "prove the offense," which in many instances equates to proving how we are required to exist? Will our destinies be determined without cultural context, a "finding" made that asserts we had "no cause to feel harmed"?

As others, if we are quiet, the risks are great. If we are not, the risks are great.

Silence is often the safer alternative to speaking, as we fear being readily labeled, stereotyped, stigmatized. Perhaps one can't be misinterpreted if one stays quiet.

I was always puzzled at how otherwise savvy individuals did not see the harm done to their businesses when they silenced and diminished voices, opting instead to model and reward conformity. The stifling of natural talent—people's ideas, creativity, and innovations, but more important, the stifling of their fundamental energy to exist and be productive—is devastating and happens every day. When business is getting only partial capability from people because too much energy must go into translation, allaying fear, fighting isolation, then how is this human loss accounted for?

I like to imagine a world where there are no ramifications when someone points out that a comment was offensive, hard to hear or even hurtful, and instead of defensiveness, the reaction is "I really want to understand that, I am sorry, and how do I . . ." or "It would really help me if you would explain why and what is behind it." I know plenty of people sitting in organizations everywhere willing to model this behavior. They need only small indicators that it is safe to behave differently— a nod or approving gesture from someone in a power seat. Otherwise, people stay silent, stay safe. Safe from disapproval, from dismissiveness, even ridicule. Shaming of the caring still permeates corporate cultures.

Culture is a top-down norm in hierarchical work organizations, so a culture of empathy is best modeled through approving and rewarding behaviors from those in power. Leaders can do what no one else can. They can choose to see. They can opt to eliminate fear from their cultural equation.

They can be receptive and accessible without losing an ounce of what they believe is their power. They can ask the right questions, such as "What can we do differently that matters for you?" "What obstacles can I help remove?" "Is there anything causing you to feel like you are not a part of things here?" "Do you feel connected to the right information and people?" "Would you like to grab lunch?" Simple questions, honest questions, valuable answers.

For hundreds of years, my community has lived with race violence as our reality. Even that statement makes many people uncomfortable, sends others into choruses of denial. Yet in a book covering just the arc of my life and career, it is present as one of the underlying themes informing the idea of "safety" for people of color, in particular Black people of America and beyond. Belonging, safety, thriving, today's terms describing how organizations function, have a disproportionate gap to fill when it comes to historical experiences of Black people. The incomprehensible circumstances of Trayvon Martin's murder in 2012 was a harbinger of a time when racist policing, violence, death, and harassment of Black men and women at the hands of police could no longer go unnoticed or contained in white spaces. Black and brown people had to fret deeply about getting safely from point A to point B, or the same for their children or loved ones. This would not, could not, stay outside of work. We brought it with us. A topic that had long ago reached a point of no return, had now erupted to a point of no ignoring. The "safe" places our coworkers may have hoped they could exist in and avoid talking or hearing about the stark realities of life while Black in America had evaporated. But business in America was ill prepared to navigate what followed.

In May 2020, the world awoke to the brutal news of a Black man murdered in Minneapolis by a law enforcement officer pressing a knee on his neck for eight minutes and forty-nine seconds, while he lay in the street dying, captured on a video the world would see. George Floyd's murder thrust race into consciousness around the world, birthing a host of statements and testimonies about how much Black Lives *did matter.*

In a world still fraught with daily racial strife and incredible gender and economic disparity, within the walls of commerce the responsibility to realign it all falls heavily, still, on those of us least represented within those same walls of commerce. It has fallen upon us to be the translators, interpreters, code-switching experts, and explainers of systems and ideologies we did not create. And as this continues to wreak havoc on our well-being, it is no surprise that some are simply opting out. My younger colleagues, mentees, and just people in general are simply refusing to continue to "understand the assignment." Refusing to demonstrate our magnificently multilingual gift of communicating. Refusing the job in addition to our jobs. The cost of our need to exert meta effort eats well into business profits, yet remains largely unacknowledged as a loss. People checking out, people using less than their full complement of talent, people suffering lowered well-being unnecessarily all are conditions representing real quantifiable loss. And the relentless, exhausting, personal cost is immeasurable.

There are still a few voices courageous enough to say to the dominant, the powerful and privileged, that if they want a high-impact future in a changing world, *they* need to able to adapt. That they will want to shape teams around new voices and learn from those new voices. That new voices require investments of open-mindedness and thoughtful ways to incorporate human and creative assets. And that it might feel like it is largely up to them to create the formula where this works, but in a thriving culture, everyone is playing a position.

In companies that understand that to see people, see talent, prepping the culture and its leaders in early stages is a critical starting point. People who truly get talent and see it, like Sue Webb, whom I worked with for years at Apple. For every candidate Sue brought in, she prepared the hiring team to see their broader dimension, expertly framing all the possible ways they'd be an asset to the business, infusing the conversation with human sparks of interest. It was never simply a sell, it was set up as a master class for all parties.

I don't have the answers leaders always want to hear, so to help them get there I have questions—for anyone leading today or who will in the future. In the place of budgeting (when that actually happens) for various and sundry diversity programs and events, what if today's leaders had individually customized coaching on being culturally competent? Coaches who'd help them see the ways they were *not* seeing? Coaching that helped them to see that human-centered work moves along a continuum, and progress along that continuum is contingent upon acknowledgment of the uncomfortable and requires more and different from them? Can we place them with the "coaches" in this world who understand they must help them see the harm and impact of their othering? To help them see beyond the linear metrics of their P&Ls and understand the science of human impact metrics? Who can help leaders of today and tomorrow see that by denying the pure biology of bias or dictating outcomes that assure their sole comfort, more harm takes place, harm they are accountable for? And within that tone of harm, the ability to innovate, create, exceed, or all inclusively thrive ultimately perishes. Who can help? Who will be allowed to help? Who might they listen to?

Chapter 10

Empathy, Misunderstood

*And then when you keep it real with people, they cross the line,
take your kindness for weakness and that's weak.*

—DRAKE, "CHARGED UP"

When I ran an ER department, people remarked on my ability to hear everyone's side of the story. I was often intent on probing for the "why," because the "why" typically revealed the very reasons we were where we were in the first place. There was, unfortunately, rarely much patience for the "why," just the desire to solve, fix, and move on.

Lack of interest in the "why" meant I spent more time than we should have unraveling and de-escalating situations. It meant I experienced resistance to leading the department in this way, as it made more room for unearthing things that people would prefer to remain undiscussed. Managers wanted uncomfortable situations to go away and felt no need or desire to revisit or think about them after a "problem" was solved. Yet there was generally much we could learn through asking the right questions: information revealed patterns, and patterns helped identify solutions. The very same managers expertly ran their businesses in this way—but it was a lot harder for them to do the same with human challenges.

When I led teams for the Apple Stores, we wanted to create enriched customer engagement, achieved through employees who were fully realized in their roles. We could not expect thousands of our employees to touch millions of customers, yet treat them casually, inauthentically, or cheaply. If that was how our employees felt, that would be exactly what customers walked away with, full stop.

This was profoundly clear to me and to members of my team, yet in those early years we had to work hard to establish this premise more broadly, and some, across various pockets of the company, never really embraced this idea as the intelligent business strategy it was. So we used Maslow's hierarchy and other premises to help people across the company understand how it all was going to work.

It took time, but the idea of purpose did eventually start to take hold. Differing somewhat from the creation and making of products, touching millions of people around the world required a guidance system, a vision . . . a reason for being. A reason to exist that valued seeing. Hearing. Serving, inspiring. The activating of purpose required thoughtfulness about how we might uplevel the day-to-day experiences of hourly employees, because if they were struggling to make their personal ends meet, or believing they were seen simply as "labor," this same transactional existence would come through to customers, to people en masse. Ultimately a diminished people experience could even diminish the products, minimizing the opportunities to create the place where Apple products first became transformative for millions of people. So we listened, and we saw them, and when they were seen, their best was returned in multiples. We listened to employees, to what they told us was important to them, directly applying what we heard, such as tuition assistance for those seeking more education, full health benefits even for part-time hourly staff, and career experiences for those who loved learning and growing. And there was mutuality. We learned also. We watched, and in seeing, learned that the people we could most rely upon to enrich others were people who loved learning, thinking, and inspiring. These were not typical traits for retail staff, these were traits that required an environment where they could thrive. With few exceptions, retailing, up until the Apple Stores were created, was a largely directed top-down, operationally hefty industry culture. That was the tried-and-true way to manage that many people and assure desired outcomes and revenue. Yet Ron Johnson topsided the notion of top-down, and we challenged ourselves to create a culture that supported people in balance with their humanity and their desire to be alive and vibrant to the never-ending foot traffic in the Stores. We had to learn how to help them continue being our greatest and most important resource. Space and time had to be created. For some, simply offering them more autonomy to relate to customers was all they needed to feel seen—something we'd learned years earlier from studying Ritz-Carlton, that autonomy could be trusted and staff would do wonderful creative things to engender connection and loyalty.

When we were increasingly successful recruiting and developing compassionate and emotionally intelligent store leaders, and in more places around the world, the culture really ignited, and in a huge way. It all worked, and it all stemmed from such a simple premise.

We'd envisioned a world where everyone—with no regard to age, background, or level of experience—could learn to use our technology comfortably, without judgment or intimidation. And we achieved this through a lens of empathy. Yes, Apple Stores were gorgeous, the products awe-inspiring, but it all worked together like voices in a choir because people—employees and customers—felt seen. Customers allowed us to become an extension of their lives; they could come visit an Apple Store, spend time with the newest Apple product, and want to stay, hang out, and just learn stuff. It was not a transaction; we had created a total experience that expanded their lives.

To perpetuate a seeing, thriving culture, we at the core of the Stores created a document containing a credo of commitments. The commitments were to uphold the vision of Apple products, strive to enrich the lives of customers, and protect in every way the resource we deemed most important: people. The commitments were indeed called a "credo," and it served as the guidance system that drove a culture of care and empathy as its standard, with an insistence upon valuing people first—their full selves, heart and soul.

One of the earliest versions of the credo stated:

At Apple our most important resource, our soul, is our people. We value dynamic, intelligent, and interesting people who are passionate about Apple. We offer a stimulating work environment, designed to create unparalleled career experiences and develop lifelong skills.

We value innovation and an environment that embraces change. We celebrate our diversity, unique talents, and passion to strengthen the brand globally. We are a community where great relationships, open communication, learning, leading, and growing serve our customers.

A years-later evolution of the same document landed upon, still, what was believed to be most important:

We believe our soul is our people.

People who recognize themselves in each other.

People who shine a spotlight only to stand outside it.

People who work to leave this world better than they found it.

People who live to enrich lives.

While these types of manifestos can be found in many organizations, they often feel like just that . . . corporate rah-rah forcibly presented to employees to remind them what to say or how to feel. There seemed to be, however, something very authentic that resonated with people around these sets of statements. It may have been the collection of leadership figures that the employees first heard the statements from—Ron Johnson, myself, Steve Cano, Duke Zurek, Carol Monkowski, Linda Turner, Art Diaz, Laura Wynn—all figures employees believed, even revered. It might have been impactful that these statements were delivered both in format and with a level of authenticity not frequently witnessed in corporate sales functions. It might have simply been impactful because of the absolute sincerity emanating from them. A document not authored by a PR department, but by a collective representation of employees from every corner of the retail business. The document was treated not as a mandate, but as inspiration to a north star that illuminated the path to thriving. It felt very human, even to me, a coauthor of the earliest versions of it, and a frequent orator of its most important lines about people.

Employees referenced these words in multiple ways, and in so doing, affirmed daily the truth of the words of the credo. That people, as the soul of a business this complex, were truly the not-very-secret sauce of why it worked. We opted not to shy away from the "soft" language that made some people uncomfortable. Prioritizing humanity enabled us to attract likeminded, emotionally smart people the world over. Staff and teams across the company worked tirelessly to bring together this human-fueled vision. Codifying and actively using a credo as an overarching guidance system allowed people in suburban regions of the world to feel as seen as the teams in Tokyo, London, Shanghai, New York, Sydney, or San Francisco.

I've always said we create culture by design or by default—nothing around us magically takes shape without either intent or lack of intent. What we created years ago at Apple happened not by accident but through deliberate, meticulous design. We created a movement of serving, gathering, and focus on the human experience, something we now see across the retail industry by chains that emulated, in full or in part, the people-focused, immersive experience Apple started.

Whether I knew them personally or not, I can typically spot someone who served in leadership with us in that early era of launching our first Stores. Steve Cano was hand-picked to open Stores in NYC, Palo Alto, and then Japan, ultimately becoming chief of Stores across the world. A great friend to this day, he remains one of the kindest humans I know. Stephanie Fehr was the creator of PhD-level leadership competencies that found a home in the lexicon of every store leader in every country. And then there were just fundamentally, profoundly human-centered people: Duke Zurek, who passionately represented Minnesota; Wendy Beckman was a force from NYC, then to the whole of Europe; Carol Monkowski reigned in the Midwest; and Gary Hutcherson, with his U.S. Marine background, led Apple Stores in Japan through an earthquake and tsunami with heroism and humanity.

These leaders and others they raised up used a different language. They modeled authenticity and applied empathy. They understood being present, and took the time to do so, and in the complex regions of markets they led, managed to stay singularly attuned to their teams. I watched them all firsthand as we built teams across the world with the same attributes. We inspired one another to stay accountable and focused on this mission. It mattered. Often I'll run across my former colleagues, or someone hired and trained by them, and it is apparent they moved forward with these values, as they remain hugely successful in business and in life. They continue to see, as they were seen.

For any company who did not start out with it prioritized, I believe empathy is a must-have skill that organizations need to navigate the slow, deliberate, soul-level work of shifting to a human-focused culture, transforming an environment intent upon thriving. Empathy is essential for any industry, and any kind of work. We all must learn how to employ and apply it if we are to design and build cultures that include, that minimize "othering" and promote thriving. Empathy in action counterintuitively creates more space and time, as it collects perspective that can be readily deployed when needed.

That manager who sees and knows more about her team is better placed to address a human issue when it presents itself, and these are indeed times for the emergence of human challenges. We need to grant permission for people to be human, right alongside the goal of driving successful business outcomes. We need these concepts to be no longer separate, but inseparable. And as the reach of AI expands to assume more "machine" work, I believe we will be called into greater action to expand humanly; to both fulfill what machine learning will not achieve or push back on what we do not want it to attempt to achieve.

In an early morning phone call, a close friend of mine was furious.

"I simply can't lie down and accept the way these insurance people are dealing with Mom's simple request for more therapy," she lamented. "They don't know her, they don't know what they are doing, they are incompetent, and they need to be fired!"

"Yep, I agree," I said. "And yet, they are not very well trained, probably brand-new remote hires, or possibly even temporary workers filling urgent customer service gaps."

"They should still be fired; they are rude and insensitive and not solving Mom's issue."

"I know. They likely aren't trained to solve, only to minimally respond. They are probably making seven dollars an hour or something ridiculous."

"Why are you defending them? It is not okay!" she said, her ire increasing by the moment.

"I'm not defending, just trying to offer you a perspective that might lessen your frustration."

"You always do this, though; you always defend people, and people need to be accountable for their actions!"

My friend is a serious-minded professional, struggling with elder care and post-pandemic levels of customer service. She was not interested in empathizing with the people placing barriers in the way of her mother's medical needs. I was probably not helpful in that moment, but she did text later to thank me and apologize, and then called again to say more.

She felt that my sharing insight into who the workers were, and their likely lack of training, was akin to absolving the insurer. That I was "over-understanding them." My comments were intended only to help her figure out where best to focus her energy, and that wasn't on the service agents. We had a good conversation on how, for her, my tendency to seek context translated to forgiveness of wrongdoing. From my perspective, I felt she often rejected information that could help her with context and help solve issues with less anxiety. Both of us heard and committed to better seeing each other's perspective. She said, "I get it . . . but it bothers me sometimes when you do this. You are just too understanding, and I want people to pay!" she said without remorse.

I told her I'm not nice at all, but that seeing the full picture of a situation allowed me to study how and where to focus my revenge strategy! This at least made her laugh.

This is the mistaken image of empathy, which is too often seen as "nice" instead of as a strategic chess board advantage, an essential skill for the twenty-first century. I hope this is shifting and people are figuring out how to talk about empathy and the power and strength it wields. I have—obviously—long been a believer in empathy; a book I gave to my leaders in HR was *Applied Empathy* by strategist and design firm CEO Michael Ventura. Ventura opens the book with: "Empathy is a squishy word . . . confused with sympathy and mistaken for being nice." A friend initially gave me this book and said, "Here are your words, but a CEO is saying them."

There are now volumes of books and articles written on the need for empathy and how to develop it. But in *A Whole New Mind,* Daniel Pink talks about how the entire medical profession has begun its shift from detached concern to empathy. Psychiatrist and medical ethicist Jodi Halpern has been a leading voice for this movement: "Doctors were trained to believe that emotional detachment from patients is personally and professionally necessary, but experience shows that patients don't trust doctors who are aloof or superficially friendly. Yet only recently have studies proven how harmful detachment and how beneficial empathy is for healing." Second only to my own personal experiences, I cannot come up with a more compelling endorsement for business sectors also to make a deliberate cultural shift to lead with empathetic sensibility.

In their highly regarded manual for the emotional quotient (EQ), *Emotional Intelligence and Your Success,* the authors Steven Stein and Howard Book discuss why such a powerful tool as empathy is so underutilized. They cite three main reasons: First, it is confused with being nice, polite, or pleasant (and the fact that businesspeople eschew this tagline is also telling). We live in an era where people simply have no interest in what is perceived as civility. Second, it is confused with sympathy and the act of giving comfort. Finally, it is believed to be a show of agreement or approval of a position not agreed with or approved. Are business leaders resistant to demonstrating empathy for these reasons? For fear that they might be mistaken for nice, polite, comforting, or supportive? May heaven forbid.

In my residency at Cornell Tech, I presented to department deans *Six Essential Considerations for Inclusive Tech Leadership,* my residency findings for faculty after the first year spent on the campus. I named empathy as key to building inclusivity, belonging, and thriving. Presented as the new "hard" skill, recommending empathy as essential in developing technology that engages humanly. As I was creating this document, I spent a lot of time with bright graduate students, discussing their preparation for future roles as next-gen technology leaders and creators. I was heartened by their thoughtfulness and very human-focused conversations. Yet when it was time to pitch their ideas and new apps and technologies to faculty, I noted the same students appeared to be reticent to acknowledge empathy, almost as if the bench of professors they faced might view it with less value.

I recognized this conditioning, and I hoped my recommendations to prioritize empathy would help them feel more courageous about leading with it. And now, after a worldwide pandemic that has forever impacted our collective understanding of everything about being human, our eyes seem to have been opened to the fact that in every possible area, sector, industry, or institution, *more* is needed. More humanity. Absolutely more empathy, but also more permission to exert our humanness.

. . .

At the end of employee meetings, Tim Cook would open the floor for employees to ask questions. A young Hispanic man once jubilantly raised his hand and said, "Thank you, I'm so happy to be here. I love working at Apple, and I want to do more in my career, and I wonder if you could share with us your ideas about mentor programs and who were your mentors?"

Tim paused, always comfortable with silence. He responded by saying, "I like to learn from everybody. I never really believed in mentor programs, but I guess they are good for some. I just think we learn from everyone." A sound and honest response. Tim's experience, as I knew it, had been as an accomplished, highly regarded professional for the entirety of his career. I wish he'd understood that in that moment a young man with a very different background and demographic had the courage, in front of thousands of employees also listening for his response, to ask this most powerful CEO about mentoring—and that meant he really needed and was seeking a mentor.

I wish that leaders who sit at the tops of organizations and who enjoy significant success without having named mentors, or who are connected enough to have an entire network of mentors, better understood the experience of having no access, no networks, no social structures or cultural cues that would help them learn the inner workings of a company. Nothing. There are people within the walls of your organizations who get nothing. No insight, no information, no counsel. There are people in organizations who slip, unseen, through well-intended infrastructure.

I wish more leaders understood this to be one of the biggest gaps to having a "bench" of diverse representation moving up and into decision-making levels in companies. There are still too many pockets of places where people can remain unseen, because they have no access, no inside information or insight, no mentors, no "help." Smart and talented people can be found among and alongside staff working security and at call centers, data centers, and retail stores.

An empathetic conversation with the lowest-level employees in any given organization will tell a story and offer a robust picture of what a C-level executive needs to understand about seeing people, starting with the fact that they need and want to actually *be* seen—and have an opportunity to learn something from the most influential people in the organization. Almost everyone wants this. It is not limited, not exclusive.

If asked that same mentoring question that Tim Cook had addressed, I hope a chief executive would say, "I was never fortunate enough to have a specific mentor in my career, so I learned in other ways and from lots of people, but I would love to hear from you what your ideal mentor program would look like." Such a response might convey to a young employee that not only was it a good idea to ask, but there may be an opportunity for him to help shape a mentoring program for himself and others.

After every major Apple Store opening, our leadership team would gather briefly before grabbing a flight to the next destination. The openings were only the beginning of a long weekend of meeting, greeting, and introducing new stores to their new communities; to large crowds of delighted customers, who often still line up for hours for their first glimpse of the famed Store designs and the wonderland of Apple products.

Bob Bridger would often say to me, "You are amazing how you make this all come together; it's like magic how our people make everything we do, work!" Bob and his teams designed and built the Stores, and in many circles are revered as much as those who designed the products. Given Bob's exceptional background and street cred within Apple's design culture, his compliment was flattering, and I knew he meant it sincerely. But it overlooked the actual professional skills of my team, which were not magical, but highly effective human systems work. My more reflective concern was that these kinds of compliments, though lovely, downplayed the need for all teams to apply empathy to their work, as it isn't something uniquely "human resources" related but simply uniquely *human*.

I recall responding to Bob: "None of this happens by any special magic of mine, as much as I'd love to claim that. My teams expend the same level of effort and skill as yours do. Yours build and design, and so do mine, except our design brief starts with how to care and ends with how to thrive."

"I get that," the consummate builder of iconic stores responded.

That's it; that is all I believed it required. My only magic had come from not separating myself from my upbringing, which taught me much about seeing people and how to care about what I saw, the way I believe Dr. Halpern hopes doctors will do with patients. I was given an opportunity in my role at Apple to inspire thousands to see millions. A veritable chain reaction of seeing people, with empathy, insight, and intelligence. This happened not because I or we were "nice," but because we sought out the traits of emotional intelligence, we prioritized empathy, and in leaders, we required compassion. The level of intention found in our employee and leadership training was undeniable, and the talented functional experts on my team devoted time, investment, and high-level expertise to this work. It was serious, hard work that required them all to see people. It was demanding work, but in looking back at it and reflecting on the fact that it is still direly needed, it's clear to me it was the most important work of our lives.

Our current world demands a new skill profile, for leading and, honestly, just for existing, if we are to survive these chaotic times. Facing ourselves and the darker parts of our day-to-day humanity is hard. Understanding how we got to where we are is hard. Yet here we are. If we are to engage with each other in any possible way forward, we have to start with empathy—as a skill, not as an excuse. Leading with it will open us, require us to be vulnerable and uncomfortable. It will not offer ready answers. We don't enjoy discomfort, and we do want ready answers. But what we will learn, if we allow it for ourselves, is how to see others and, in the seeing of others, better see ourselves.

Chapter 11

Blind, Biased, and Missing the Point

*I feel free when I see no one
and nobody knows my name.*

—LANA DEL REY, "GOD KNOWS I TRIED"

When I briefly left Apple to work at a promising startup, then a second one, the experiences were a fascinating study of organizational behavior. There were days when it felt like a textbook graduate school experience. It offered much quicker cycle times for product to market; it tested every human behavior, and sometimes tested my own.

The first company was led by a quiet, reserved CEO, a rambunctious set of founders, myself as its first official HR director, and new, more strategic and experienced engineering leadership. The technology was excellent, and things progressed fast into talks of an IPO or acquisition. As often occurs, a new CEO was hired, formerly from Oracle. We'd recruited impressive talent and had built enough infrastructure to secure more funding. However, even though I believed I'd accomplished a lot in my short time with them, I was feeling like my work was of little value to the new CEO, focused as he was on next-level viability for the technology. Oracle's intense culture, where he had been high flying, was legendary, and I made assumptions about him immediately. After a few initial meetings, I sensed little room for shifting his opinion of me, or what I thought his opinion of me was.

I attended the new CEO's first all-hands meeting, which included VCs and board members. One of our VC partners knew me quite well, and I noticed him watching me. After the meeting he approached me and asked, "What is going on with you, my friend? Every time you are around our new CEO, I see you shrinking. You seem to sink into a shell, and I don't like seeing that. That's not the person I know you to be."

I had fallen out of alignment with my core beliefs, my strength. I had become consumed with the behaviors and affectations of this individual, the new CEO, and what I believed he thought of me. I pulled back, no longer comfortable presenting the more authentic version of myself, instead behaving as a shadowy version of me. So, in a rather convoluted dynamic, I was not seeing him, but projecting what I thought he saw in me. When we become detached from our core, when we aren't asking ourselves the right questions, this can happen. I came close to deciding to walk away, even resigning, because I did not want to feel what I was feeling, but I was causing it myself. The result was me shrinking away from myself. I know now that it was not him—the issue was me. He was aggressive, but respectful, and in hindsight I saw where he did try to engage with me. But *I* did not see *him*. I projected the myths of Oracle's harsh culture onto him. At its best, seeing is a mutual action. We see each other, or we try to. But sometimes perceptions of power or predetermined ideas cloud our vision.

I'm still not entirely certain how or when I shied away.

Was it instantly, given his in-your-face style? Was it after I'd learned more of his background and extensive qualifications? What were my biases when I heard he was hugely successful, and had a fascinating Israeli upbringing including military service at age fourteen? How effective could I be with him in a lead HR role? Why was I fearful, and of what exactly?

Oracle at that time had suffered a negative reputation for their treatment of people, specifically of women, and I absorbed and projected that narrative versus seeing him for myself. I blocked his view with my preconceived judgments, and although my career did not suffer, in hindsight, I could have learned much from him and likely developed a solid relationship. I succumbed to what in research is known as "confirmation bias," the tendency we all have to embrace information that supports our beliefs and reject information that contradicts them.

Our brains are powerful. We build intricate stories in our minds, and we absorb these untested stories as truths. We make assumptions. We are quick to label a boss too critical, a coworker difficult, a friend disloyal. But these rapidly formed thought patterns can block opportunities for more truth-filled connection.

There are upward of 175 types of bias, from unconscious bias to optimism bias, and research tells us that blind spots and bias cannot be eliminated from the human mind. They exist and will be stealth and looming. They're shaped by our families, our cultural cues, our deepest psychological strengths and fears. They are powerfully applied by our mind's air traffic control. Our only hope of conquering the plethora of biases is to acknowledge and know they exist, be vigilantly aware of them and develop the discipline to confront them. To not shame ourselves for having them, but rather to try to manage them by questioning their existence. We can coexist with biases and not allow them to pilot our lives.

I did not pause to recognize my own lack of sight about the new CEO. I made decisions about him and about how I would manage him, from a place of partial blindness, which sunk into a kind of fear. I closed my eyes to seeing, to better navigate the discomfort. In this sense, biases render us sight impaired, seeing only what our minds allow us to see. But we can make a choice to understand our own biases. Doing so is another way of enhanced *seeing*—in this case, to better see ourselves.

I was working with a renowned strategy firm on an important Apple project, when I realized the collaboration was feeling slightly awkward. At the close of a week of working together, the firm's president told me his team wanted to rethink how to work with me. This was disconcerting, as they were an exciting and reputable firm. They frequently mastered the working styles of high-level execs and felt I was not responding to their presentation in the ways they'd expected me to. They were accustomed to preparing for their pitch presentation with heavy executive critique; from there, they'd rework ideas. This cycle might repeat several times until the executive was pleased enough with the presentation to fully endorse the work. Because of the cycles, this approach often cost more, or at minimum required a heavier lift from the firm, and a delicate balance of cost consciousness, creativity, and caution.

I, on the other hand, was not so interested in showing up to have them present to me a finished concept. I loved the process. I wanted to cocreate with them and with my team. We had the benefit of a room full of great minds, and I saw how all of them could contribute to a brilliant outcome, extending and enhancing the vision. I wanted to fully see and utilize everyone and give them the freedom to act on all the possibilities that arose. I'd envisioned a merged creative collaboration.

When the firm recognized this, their principal and founder met with me and said:

"We got together to regroup. It became clear that we had been approaching you as other executives in our client base, even other CHROs [chief human resources officers] we work with. We realized you were not them, nor like them. We allowed your title, reputation, and successes to determine how we'd engage with you. We are going to shift course and engage with you as an artist, as a cocreator of this new thinking."

At some level the plot twist here was that the firm had seen themselves in me. They realized I wanted to cocreate, not dictate. They saw me and the artistic perspective I worked from, not the traditional executive I'd not allowed myself to morph into. They course corrected, and we began having the most gratifying work sessions together. Our work felt aligned and vision informed. We'd seen each other in time to salvage and enhance both the relationship and the work outcome.

Claudia was my very first best friend. I don't remember ever not knowing her, which I think is how some people experience a sibling. Our parents were neighbors and friends. We could see into one another's front windows—big picture windows that, unless the draperies were closed, allowed us to see into the lives we lived. This was a metaphor for our friendship, from the time we were mere toddlers.

My earliest memories of Claudia—or "Little Claudia," as we called her, because her mother shared the same name—are of birthday parties. We began celebrating together in our early years, always with some form of chocolate cake, in her kitchen in December for her birthday, and in my backyard in June for mine. We laughed freely and cried deeply from the times of our earliest life experiences. From jacks, hopscotch, backyard playhouses, sewing class, and board games to Barbies, we were inseparable. Throughout all our life "firsts" (she was first to get a Barbie Dreamhouse) to first crushes (I had the first crush, in second grade), to who got a period first, who got to wear heels, who first wore an afro, which of us initiated more high school shenanigans, up through marriages and babies. My son, Ian, and her daughter, Brandi, were born only two years apart and were sure to marry each other, or so we hoped.

As with any relationship that long and close, we had our challenges. I thought she was intensely beautiful and complex, often moody, and not always so kind to others. She thought I was utterly brilliant, a bit of a snob, and too kind, especially with my mother or with boyfriends. Over the years we separated for college, jobs, relationships, then came back together when a relationship soured or a child was born. Our continued childhood birthday tradition of "gifting" a greeting card with a crisp one-dollar bill in it made us giggle well into our forties.

We loved so many of the same things: fashion, tomato juice and tequila shots, collard greens, music from vibraphonist Roy Ayers to activist poet Gil Scott-Heron, books, especially by Nikki Giovanni or Dick Gregory, mural art, the best eye rolls (she won), the best curse words (I won), and a shared disdain for fake and arrogant people. We never strayed far from a shared understanding of life; we would seek the other out for sanity checking, talking for hours on end on any given situation. We would always balance celebrating one another with telling the truth of how we saw things, no matter how painful. It was the most committed, truest form of friendship I'd experienced in life. We made each other better people, constantly, throughout our lives.

When my mother died in 2006, it was Claudia who stood beside me to first view her for her wake and burial. She had known my mother intimately and knew her complexity all too well. She held my hand and spoke softly. We inspected her, from suit and hair to gloves, and decided Mom would approve.

"Margaret would love how she looks. You did really really well!"

"Are you sure? You know how picky she is, and I don't want her fussing or cussing at me from beyond." Giggles. Then tears. Then a promise.

"I am here for you to bury your mother, and you must promise to be with me when the time comes for mine."

"Of course."

We were adults, still as bonded as we'd always been, when Claudia experienced a dramatic forced career shift, causing her to have to leave the airline industry. She was a longtime successful flight attendant, and the airline bureaucracy had displaced her, but she landed well on her feet in a new service industry. Soon after, she was hit with fibromyalgia. I was there, researching it, trying to help her solve each new problem the disease perpetrated, working through each issue as they came at her. Or so I thought.

As close as we were, I missed so much. I missed the true agony of her illness. I thought I was seeing and hearing her when she would call to tell me how the doctors and insurance people treated her as if she were feigning the level of pain she was in. This disbelief is a well-documented fact and a resounding deficit in health care for Black women, and I knew this professionally and personally. Yet I missed the depth of her embarrassment, her disappointment. I sometimes sent funds to help with bills, sometimes flew in just to see her in person. I held on to the stance of her bouncing back, convincing her she could get back on her feet, because I simply could not see and did not want to see her any other way.

I missed that she did not herself believe that she could bounce back up, that she was not getting the right kind of help. I missed how deeply her spirit was damaged, how deeply every hurdle harmed her.

It was February 2009, and I was in London on business, when I got the call from her younger sister Janice: "We lost Claudia."

"What do you mean we lost her? Where is she?" I pictured her getting in her car and running away, driving somewhere and not telling anyone, fleeing from pain or trouble.

She had done just that.

I remember collapsing on the floor of the hotel lobby I was standing in. My next memory, from a semi-hysterical state, was my work colleagues Karl, Sue, and Stephanie stewarding me safely onto my flight from Heathrow, now stopping in Colorado instead of home to San Francisco.

I stood as squarely as I could to sing "The Wind Beneath

My Wings" at Claudia's memorial services. I looked at her beautiful daughter, Brandi, and her family, an extension of my family that I'd known for decades, and I was able to summon the strength to sing. As we often do, inside I assumed responsibility for what was happening. I second-guessed every interaction, every phone call. How had I missed so profoundly what was now apparent? How could I have called myself her closest friend and not seen or felt her contemplation of this decision?

Over time I landed at an emotional compromise. Perhaps there was no way I could have known of her plans. In retrospect, I now understand that I had seen her the way I wanted to and helped her the way I thought best. I had a filter, a blind spot that supported what I needed from her. I needed her to be able to see her path toward healing and restoration. I needed her to be okay—for me.

I now believe Claudia knew this, knew I was seeing her future only from my view, a view where she recovered and returned to her life. She needed me to see from where *she* sat, see that she was truly tired, and have me sit with her in her truth, not mine.

For the next few years, I vowed to take a second look at the lenses I used when seeing others, especially those closest to me. Given my strong inclination to lead and influence, when it came to my family and friends, I decided to try to take a step back. To try seeing them in the way they wanted to be seen, and really needed to be seen, especially by me. To process how that was different from my vision for them. To try giving help in the ways they requested, not in the ways I believed was needed. To ask more questions, listen more deeply, to the spoken and unspoken.

Just as we'd promised, I was there years later when it was time for Claudia's mother to transition. I stood in Claudia's place, and I knew she was pleased that we had fulfilled our promises to each other. She was still making me better and accountable even then, even when it was hardest. As a favorite psalm says, be still, and know. But also know when you have done your best.

We will always miss things, miss people, and contribute to the failing of relationships. We will not see, not acknowledge, and not understand much in our lifetimes. But the idea of continually improving this process and increasing our capacity to see is worthy of our best effort.

Chapter 12

Taxation Without Representation

And who will feed a starving sparrow?
"Not I," said the Golden Wheat.

—SIMON & GARFUNKEL, "SPARROW"

Representation matters at every level. I know when I walked into a conference room or stepped onto a platform representing Apple as a Black female executive, if there was a person of color in the room, something ignited in them. It might have been hope, optimism, pride, even comfort, but there was always a spark of recognition.

I was in my early years at Apple when a MacWorld conference was live broadcast into Café Mac for employees to watch. Viewing the event from Apple's storied Café, or any designated spot on campus, always specially equipped with large screens and wonderful sound, was a big deal and an absolute thrill for employees. It was our first look, right alongside the rest of the world, and anticipation of what was to come, as Steve and Apple engineers influenced the direction of technological existence for us all.

This day, the new iMac G4—the fun, all-in-one desktop often compared to the iconic Pixar lamp—launched with a commercial that featured the song "Stomp," a blowout contemporary gospel hit by Kirk Franklin. The iMac enthusiastically and animatedly danced to the Kirk Franklin tune. I remember watching and almost gasping when I heard the unmistakable opening lyrics "For those of you that think . . ." followed by Franklin's choir's trademark sound. I am certain I danced for a few seconds at least, then subdued myself into bopping up and down to the music. I looked around at coworkers nearby, but they were oblivious as to why I was so excited.

I knew several things the folks viewing alongside me did not. One, this recording was an absolute breakout hit within the Black community. Two, the artist, Kirk Franklin, was huge and important to us; he had accomplished something culturally significant by bringing together traditional and contemporary gospel ideology, breaking the barriers of tradition, and including more people, more joyfully, becoming a (Black) household name in the process. Third, as a member of an underrepresented group so often overlooked by the very major brands we avidly supported, I knew this ad represented an opportunity to connect Apple products to our community. I knew that the convergence of that particular music with this ad, at this moment, meant Apple could more compellingly capture the attention of our community, and that could only be a positive. In that moment I was a real-time case study on why diverse representation and cultural authenticity mattered, and how it manifests.

Feeling a bit of courageous optimism, I decided to write to Steve. Mind you, this was soon after my 2001 return to Apple, after going out and experiencing startup company adventures. So I was certainly not on day-to-day-email terms with him. I felt compelled, though. I wanted to share what I'd felt and believed was an important example of the kind of impact we could be making. I sat in my office and wrote a thoughtful note, explaining how the ad had affected me, what it meant, why I was excited about it. I copied my then-boss Dan Walker in case there were political ramifications to just trotting out a note to the famous chief. I did not expect a response from him, but I did believe he would read it. I felt the need to make sure he understood the significance of what had transpired with one well-done, well-placed creative ad. I was reasonably certain there was no one near him who'd quite understand its significance in the way I'd understood it, who'd seen and felt what I had, then convey it to him in a way I believed he'd resonate with.

True to form, however, inside of an hour Steve did respond. He thanked me for the note, for the insight, said he was not aware, thought it was a "cool song," and introduced me via the same email to the person responsible for the ad's music selection. "Hey and meet Denzyl, you guys should talk and share more ideas." I followed up on the introduction to British musicologist and producer Denzyl Feigelson. We became fast friends.

Denzyl's unique recommendation for the iMac ad stemmed from his knowledge of and love for gospel music, and from an affiliation with Malaco Records. Denzyl understood how compelling the song would be and how whimsically it would animate a computer ad. He is a knowledgeable fan of many genres, particularly ones I love and care deeply about. We spent hours over the years talking about music and conceptualizing, as he listened and often took my input. I recently did a search for this wonderful ad. It seems that the live ad no longer appears in the public domain, which is too bad since I imagine it would still be wonderful to watch. It does appear in Apple Music's chronology of music used for Apple ads over the years. Denzyl and I will always remember it, the fun, joy, charm, and what it said, knowingly or unknowingly, to a valued community. It said: We see you.

The intrinsic benefit of having multicultural people and the experiences they bring sharing input on business and product decisions seem obvious. It is much talked about as a manifestation of "diversity," but we don't hear enough real-time stories that demonstrate how these benefits manifest and how they have the power to directly impact a community. My good friend Damien Hooper-Campbell served as the first chief of DEI for Zoom Communications. Damien, a brilliant and gifted graduate of Morehouse and Harvard, reached out to me for my thoughts when he was first considering the Zoom offer, toward the beginning of the pandemic.

I told him, "This is important; you will be at the helm of the ultimate digital inclusion use case, and you can lead and model the ways the world needs to connect and become virtually inclusive." I was excited for him, as I had been teaching at Cornell Tech about the concept of digital inclusion, a term I coined to describe the virtual elements of inclusion that also needed to be at the core of any company's DEI remit.

Little did either of us know just how significantly Zoom Technologies would become culturally embedded in our pandemic norms and beyond. Noun became a verb, as we virtualized and digitized human connection, Zooming our way through those unbelievable months that led to years. The company leaders were pressed into service to exert stunning pivots and ramp-ups to support what became in that moment the world's most existential tech demand: to be able to virtually connect fully in a world where human connection was suddenly and unexpectedly cut off. Damien was an important voice behind the technology as we became heavily reliant on their products for our connections to the world. I, for one, was grateful the technologists at Zoom had Damien's perspective and humanity. He was an HBCU and Harvard Business school grad, a Black man with a multicultural background, a high EQ, and lived experiences that would help them think about how to design for and consider use cases for a world suddenly in dire need of connecting, need, versus being the enterprise meeting tool it was and before soaring to $16 billion in market value. The impact of Damien's intelligence, presence, and experiences mattered profoundly to a world in need of connection, a world that did not know Damien was there, behind the scenes, illuminating key decisions, especially as they related to unseen communities.

How do so many companies still underestimate the marketplace savvy of the very customers they serve? How do they miss how deeply representation matters to large segments of their consumers? So much missed opportunity. From multihued "flesh" colored Band-Aids to the "flesh" colors in Crayola crayons, toys, books, food, segment marketing is still broadly underrepresented inside of companies and poorly studied for cultural authenticity.

Designer brands continue to trip over themselves when they miss a cultural cue. Walmart and others somehow missed that Juneteenth "merchandise" warranted recognition of the cessation of over four hundred years of enslavement, when they launched themed picnic products that included red velvet ice cream and party banners. Were a cross section of its Black employees consulted for input, even by one member of the marketing staff? Was there any discussion on how to direct benefits to the community that Juneteenth originated from? I know employees who shared that their corporate marketing teams had never heard of the holiday, which did not surprise me, but these were the same companies that declared commitment to equity (in totality just pledges came in at around $100 billion) after the summer of Mr. Floyd's murder. Did the thought of donating a portion of profits from the sale of merchandise commemorating Black liberation, to Black organizations in Black communities ever come up as an idea for equity pledges? This uninformed thinking is likely to continue as long as the representation within companies remains in single digits, decision-makers are not engaging with the humans behind those numbers, and there aren't enough people who look like me who sit inside of companies willing to shoot an email to their CEO when they do get something right. How can representation really matter if not seen, activated, and acted upon?

In 2014, more than fifteen years after the Kirk Franklin ad ran, I worked on the Apple/Beats acquisition team. The $3 billion price tag to acquire Beats was much discussed, inside and outside of Apple. For me, a Black woman, Beats was a well-known entity, fun and relevant in the music and sports worlds, with a clear leaning toward the hip-hop community. As rumors grew, I was frequently asked about this venture, with a lilt to the inquiry implying that surely *I* would have a perspective on this unusual matching. Having made it a habit, after years at the company, to politely return inquiries about Apple business with the familiar "you see me saying absolutely nothing" response, I knew, from the number of questions coming my way, that people were increasingly curious.

I also recognized that a cultural conversation was ensuing and we needed to find a way to participate in that conversation, despite our proclivity to secrecy. We were engaging with a brand-new community, and it was not going to be okay to simply see the acquisition through and quietly absorb the Beats ecosystem into Apple. An additional line in a PR narrative also would not be sufficient. We needed to see and recognize this new community of consumers.

There was *that* moment. When rapper, producer, and Beats cocreator Dre and an all-smiles actor-singer Tyrese exuberantly discussed the Beats-Apple deal on video. "$3.2 billion from Apple, Beats just changed hip-hop!" Tyrese exclaimed to Dre, following up with the traditional pouring of brown liquor, a recognized toast in our communities. All caught on film, posted, and immediately seen by millions. I imagined I felt a bit of a tremor emanate from the San Andreas Fault beneath Cupertino. Then the video abruptly disappeared, and silence ensued.

I understood completely what had just happened and why. My corporate colleagues categorized the incident as hubris and business immaturity. However, from my view, we at Apple had just had perhaps a first public Black Moment. The magnitude of what this deal meant to the community that produced Dre and Tyrese was what that celebration was all about. They were seen—and seen by a giant like Apple. The huge price tag was notable, but this was just as much about the unprecedented ascension of who and what the Beats brand represented, significant enough for two Black icons of the culture to prematurely celebrate it.

Later, in my office with my door closed, I had my own moment of a quiet giggle. Yes, what happened had occurred in two worlds and in two dimensions. What the world saw as a fascinating billion-dollar business transaction, I saw as a cultural moment in time that could profoundly set a new tone for how companies might collaborate with communities of color—in ways no one could yet fathom. And it had just been sent into the viral stratosphere, and not by Apple.

African Americans in the United States, a population of just under fifty million, represent $1 trillion in spending power. Hispanics in the U.S., at upward of sixty-one million, hold spending power of $1.5 trillion. These very present and fast-growing communities are certainly seen for what can be extracted from them. They are yet unseen for what they offer in long-term growth, investment strategies, or meaningful community engagement.

The disparity between the lack of opportunity for Blacks working in the field of technology in contrast to our role as consumers and the trillions of dollars the Black community spends on technology, is painful insight. These are difficult conversations to have, as we find diversity teams within companies relegated to "staying in their lanes," while the kinds of decision-makers authorized to have these conversations sit at the top of companies, or in rooms of dismal representation. And when it comes to the making of decisions that might actually flow funds, significant funds, into communities versus back into the company to "reinvest," we are looking at extremely small elite circles of humans. Those who hold the power to unlock these actions that could evoke meaningful social shifts. Those who could, with no repercussion, no negative consequence. The excuses for the holding back of resources for decades could be tossed out with the same rigor used to toss out excuses for weak business practices, for a failed product or strategy. The elite decision-makers we all know sit in the rooms where it happens, can do much, much more.

"We can't find them," whatever the "them" might be, is a fallacy. It is a fallacy in recruiting. It is a fallacy with Black creators, entrepreneurs, and developers of technology that absolutely do exist and can be readily cultivated. Business and commerce find what they want, infuse and cultivate supply, then continue growing it. Black-owned businesses as suppliers to technology companies have been vying for contracts for years and have been dismissed, ignored, or funded sparsely in contrast to non-Black suppliers.

"These suppliers just aren't up to our standards" is a fallacy. Of course they are not, as opportunity and access have not been made available to them. Companies can simply decide to develop, fund, support, and enhance Black and brown suppliers. Full stop.

Companies can decide to disperse their millions more equitably in advertising budgets. Companies can cross reference the equity pledge they made in the wake of summer 2020 with the minuscule percentages of their actual spend on Black communities, and contrast it to what they earn from Black spending on their products.

So as decision-makers continue to fail to see both the connection (or disconnection) between what is being promised and what is possible, and the uncomfortable truth of why this obnoxious gap is still allowed to exist, we make the same statements, the same apologies. And for much of corporate America, the cheaper bet is still, in this advanced time, to buy the table at the annual local NAACP fundraiser for $30k rather than invest $500k in the infrastructure of a Black-owned supplier of plastic encasements or fund the cost of expanded truck leasing for a Hispanic-owned dry-cleaning service. When innovation is everywhere, AI is leaping and bounding, and every other business process is advanced, how do we justify this continued failure to see these systemic issues around dismal representation? Is it the fear of shareholder challenges? If enough companies began taking these actions, the market would adjust itself and shareholders would continue to share wealth. I believe most thinking people understand, by now, that this is a much deeper challenge, and we are indeed up to our collars in deep challenges these days.

My friend Seth Goldenberg, author of *Radical Curiosity,* originated the phrase "unlearning as a form of activism." Unlearning is a decision, a commitment, and a decidedly active way to resist a future of sameness, of excusing away the failure to see. Consider unlearning as a pathway to better vision, faster change, and finally closing gaps, because, I promise you, you can unlearn.

Chapter 13

Sing Your Own Song

This is my story, this is my song.

—FANNY CROSBY,
"BLESSED ASSURANCE"

My former boss Dan Walker called me one day, when we were a decade into creating Apple Stores around the world.

"Congratulations," he said, "you are famous. You, Stephanie, Sean, and Sue—all of you guys are famous for what you've done at Apple. You are being written up everywhere, and it is business history."

I adored Dan, but I did not believe anything had been written up, or that we as a team had reached some notable level of recognition. I did know the global impact of the work we'd done, and its effect on customers, by now in the millions, and on employees. I especially knew people whose lives had changed as a result of working in a retail store. People whose trajectory was altered because they felt purpose and meaning, because they were allowed to learn. I did know that we had created a culture where human beings in the many thousands were thriving, and that they believed they were contributing to a better world. I knew this because these same people shared it with me, with us, daily.

I'd established meaningful relationships around the world, from New York to London to Fukuoka. I'd encountered truly special people, engaged with them, advocated for them. I'd scoffed at their surprise at having access to me, to someone at "my level." I believed my level was there to see and support their ability to thrive, for without them, my level would be meaningless.

However, I began to realize—before Ron Johnson's departure, Steve's death, and Tim's ascendance—that this was not a repeatable experience for me. I had no aspirations for a bigger job or title; that was not how I moved through life. Rather, I sought out greater meaning.

My artist soul had been trying hard to emerge. Musically, I am a natural soprano. As the highest voice on the scale, a soprano voice can be heard for its power or its delicacy. It is distinguishable, it is unique. And although it had taken years in various stages of my life to truly understand the breadth of that voice, I knew I had it. I kept my art close to me in various ways. From a young age I had always envisioned a circle of creative friends with whom I would create, inspire, learn from, and share, and this idea had found its way back into my psyche.

My parents died in 2004 and 2006. Not long after that, my son's father, Daniel, passed, as well as my best friend, Claudia. During that time of grieving, I found myself back in the Fifth Avenue Apple Store in New York, where I ran into a stunning Black man, impeccably dressed, almost from another time. He stopped and asked me the location of something he needed. I told him I worked for Apple but was not familiar with what he needed at the Store, and while awaiting assistance, we began to chat. Barry was a classical music voice coach, affiliated with the Met Opera, a publicist, and a performing baritone himself. We talked for a spell and exchanged numbers.

That meeting led to an artistic assessment from his publicist lens, some focused voice coaching, and long and candid discussions about Black people in classical music; that we bring into it a style, perspective, and vibrancy that was exciting to consider. I wondered how, as I sat firmly in my corporate life, I might incorporate some of that world into mine, resuming what I'd intended to start years prior. He could not know it at that time, but our meeting, and all that ensued, would assuage my grief at a time when the huge losses in my life had taken my breath away. As is often the case, I did not fully realize the depth of the sadness I was navigating at the time, as I continued leading a team of thousands around the globe.

But I recognized something compelling about Barry's world. It represented something I believed I could still possibly achieve, albeit not the way I might have at twenty-five, but as an artist with something to say, in my own voice. I worked earnestly with him for months, meeting in NYC whenever possible. I practiced and rehearsed incessantly. I had no end game; the process was simply life affirming. Then, one day Barry invited me to sing at one of his concerts. It was at Carnegie Hall's Weill Recital Hall and would serve as my debut performing true operatic repertoire, two Puccini arias.

Spiritually, Daniel was always with me when I performed. Many years after we parted ways, he eventually did marry and had two girls, our son Ian's half-sisters. We were all close—the girls' mother, Daniel, my family, and Ian—a modern family of sorts. I loved who Danny had become in life and loved the dreams he held on to for himself. We *saw* each other still, but we knew that we were best shooting for our own stars.

Daniel had died of complications of a stroke, while playing music, and as so often happens in life, I had to choose between two compelling, competing life events. The funeral service in his hometown coincided with the week of my invitation to perform at Carnegie Hall. It was the performance I had been training for since age fifteen when my church choir director illuminated for me what my voice was all about.

I knew Daniel deeply enough to not even debate the decision. Each time I'd lament it I could hear him saying, "Are you kidding? I am always here with you, and with Ian . . . go to New York and get on that stage and don't even think twice." But it was incredibly emotional explaining to Ian why I would not be attending his father's funeral. Ian, gently emerging into young adulthood, accepted my decision but was still profoundly hurt by it. His heart could not conceive of me not being there, especially after we had recently lost both of my parents.

I felt my son's pain, much as I carried my own, and some guilt as well. I believed, though, that the best way for me to honor our significant loss was to sing through it and allow it to inform the music. I did just that, knowing I could do so because two decades ago Ian's dad had seen me so clearly and deeply, and it had changed my life forever.

I walked into my first Carnegie appearance in a navy blue Robert Danes gown, wearing my locs styled into a crown atop my head, all golden and powerful. I was seen, and I was heard, and I took all who had gotten me there along with me.

I realized at this point that I needed music fully back in my life. I could feel it pushing breath back through me. I had been feeling out of sync for some time. When I am off center, the first indication is a loss of good breath, replaced by shallow, skimming breathing. When I stay there too long I become diminished, I fail to thrive. If instead I use the calming technique of inhaling slowly, then exhaling even more so, I can assess, listen, see more clearly. Then I can usually gather enough perspective in the moment to take my next steps, whatever they may be. Sometimes they are not physical steps at all, but simply a need to pause and be. Breathe, and allow myself to be seen and not pull away, not shrink back into a crevice only to fall further away from my core.

After the performance, I made a vow to myself to never again stop singing, at this level, with this degree of commitment. In years prior to this critical turning moment, I had many singing engagements. I belonged to an ensemble that regularly performed at the mission in Santa Clara. I performed when asked, for special events, such as a tribute to Dr. Cornel West at San Jose State University. I was half of the jazz duo Williams and Smith, with the late Marty Williams on piano. Marty took my classically oriented sound and created space for it in jazz ballads. I made time for opportunities to perform that counterbalanced my day-to-day corporate existence.

Yet after the well-received Carnegie performance, I committed differently. I placed myself in the mode to be able to deliver high-level professional performances, and when I accepted a commitment, I'd go into a training mode, devoting my time away from work, evenings, weekends, and days off to far more serious performance preparation: voice coaching, learning repertoire, rehearsing, eating properly, protecting my instrument. This became my way of refocusing my life and its relationship to my art. I was very much still the executive and committed to my responsibilities, just passing on the "drinks and working dinner" life to a great degree. My closest Apple colleagues knew of my dual life, genuinely supporting and encouraging it.

Others, when they learned I sang at a professional level, would casually ask me to break a note and prove it, right then and there, or proceed to tell me about their daughter who sings, or their neighbor on *So You Think You Can Dance*. It seemed hard to process my holding a powerful corporate role yet toggling back and forth into serious performing. I sometimes took on their concerns—how could I do both, and do them well?

Workplaces are an amalgamation of people who have come together to create, produce, serve, build. People are beautifully multidimensional; none are the same. This is a good thing. Yet it is hard for companies to see this bonus dimension of being human as the tremendous asset it is, and perhaps even learn how to not just accept it, but leverage and even lead with this advantage. It is a bit like a science experiment: Identify and isolate the cultural properties that compel people to create, write, dance, design. Create the space for people to get messy, to be themselves, to eschew titles and labels. Curate and design an environment that motivates, encourages, elevates. Do what artists and repertoire teams at record companies once did for artists: Create the best possible surroundings and conditions for them to create and thrive and insist that what is good for people is good for the enterprise. And as much as I can hear my logic-based colleagues sigh, citing systems, processes, and operating efficiencies, their worlds could be much enhanced with the addition of human-powered creativity, more risk-taking, and a sense that they can, with people-led thinking, meet every objective, thriving as they do so.

In 2012, I formed my own production company, Blue Organza Productions. I named it after the impossibly poofy dress my mother would put me in to sing. Church, party, social, whatever special event, I was in that blue organza dress, and it meant business when I wore it. It always did kind of wear me more than I wore it. I formed this LLC with the idea of a holding place for all my creative ideas: songs, writings, mentoring for up-and-coming creators, and a future recording studio. It was serious enough for me to have made the legal department at Apple aware of it to make sure there were no conflicts of any kind, but it was still just my place for the parking of ideas I had developed over years. It would lure me forward and likely away and out of corporate living. In hindsight, it was also a catharsis, as we all managed through Steve's death in 2011 in personal and collective ways.

I'm familiar with the psychological term that describes the attachment we have when a beloved public figure dies (parasocial grief), but this was so much more than that syndrome. A part of my role was to attend to those multitudes of folks who did not know him personally but whose grief was immense. Employees, their families, consumers all mourned deeply and experienced losing Steve as they would have with any close family member. This was a moment when people did see one another, offering comfort, assurances, and reflections. Apple's leadership were managing their own personal grief, in ways none of us could ever understand. In my role, I was a safe place for people closer to my level in the company to discreetly express themselves and their grief, and I was moved by it all.

It was a seismic shift in the world, and the void was unfathomable. Like a loved one within a family, Steve was profoundly loved by scores of people who worked at his company, whether or not they'd known him personally, been in the halls or auditoriums for his breathtaking keynotes, had Infinite Loop sightings, or had less-than-pleasant encounters we all knew might occur for anyone at any time. It did not matter; it all turned into a life force that I believe to this day was one of the most important transformational eras of its time, as it allowed Apple to continue transforming the world.

At Apple, the immediate collective commitment to stoically placing one foot in front of the other was as much a testimony to who Steve was as it was to Tim's moving into his own destiny with quiet nobility. The day-to-day priority was to steer a focused and steady way forward through the unspeakable. For weeks and months I watched people deal and not deal with the realities of what this all meant to them, deeply, personally, and professionally.

In the months to come, it was fascinating to navigate this transition as the world watched. Apple University had been famously created years prior to help us convey what made Apple, Apple, but people came to me constantly for help with their own desire to understand what to do now. The product leadership was so strong, there was no concern for anything but executing the vision already in place. What I observed instead was a need for reassurance, a need to know futures were assured, but more urgently, that identities were intact. There was much quiet discussion about the differences in style, a different vision, and some chat about what success might look like between the two chiefs. I mostly helped people focus on what was in front of them and advised them to trust the process of people doing the best they could. That was what we had before us, and it deserved our best.

There was no shortage of opinions on what was or was not good for the company, and a reasonable measure of fear of the unknown. Given the carefully crafted external narrative and the very clear directive from leadership to stay focused, I became a safe place for employees to express abject concerns, fears, and of course, ongoing grief. Staying focused on the big picture of Apple proved challenging for some, which we didn't yet fully understand. I was once again translator and interpreter. This time, navigating very human emotion from all kinds of people, all levels of jobs and roles, through one of the most prominent CEO transitions in modern history.

Months passed, and Tim would ask me, "Will you help me out and take over HR and talent for the entire company? I want you to do what you've done in retail for the rest of the company." I felt affirmed, but less than enthusiastic. I had been at the company for eighteen years, and I saw the top-talent position through my own lens: heavily administrative, no artistry, inordinate amounts of responsibility without a lot of clarity as to how one was evaluated. People were messy, and—still—that was a fact that not always translated well at the top of any company. I remember telling Tim, "I am an out-there-with-the-people kind of girl. I like being where the interaction is, where our products can be transformative in the moment. I love that. I don't love ivory tower life."

He laughed and said, "We're going to make sure it doesn't feel like that."

Before my father passed away, he told me, "Make sure to save and invest your savings. Don't work too long beyond being young enough to enjoy your life and do the things that you want to do." He said this after leaving a lifetime of public service, as his own health started to decline. "Don't do what I did; I waited too late."

In the moments Tim Cook was talking to me about the expanded role of HR chief, I could hear my father's words ringing clearly in my head. I felt Dad's presence at that moment. And I was certain he'd not approve of what I did next.

I said yes, fully believing I could rationalize accepting Tim's offer by establishing a few key things to accomplish, and then departing. This would ensure that I did not internalize the job as a career pinnacle nor as a long-term assignment. Of course, it was exhilarating to believe I could be effective and valuable at the C-level of the world's most admired tech company, and in that moment I did believe that I was seen for my achievements to date. I respected Tim's reasons for asking me, but I still had an overwhelming sense of having been diverted from my own personal mission of living a creative life, mentoring those coming behind me, and becoming an agent of change for the world on my own terms.

A few years earlier, I had been promoted to the vice president level in a job I had been doing for years. My ascension was unprecedented. There had been no African Americans at VP level at Apple. I was a first, to be followed by a still too small number, but others did come. Now, as it appeared from the outside, a woman, a Black woman, would head all HR and talent for Apple, at C-level. It took a minute, but I understood what this meant. *Business Insider* even published a piece: "Denise Young Smith will be responsible for Apple's most important asset, its talent."

I'd re-enlisted, and I had suited up. For me, it meant immediately assessing the role and how to approach it, my team, my colleagues, and my peers. This was the work of an executive. No time to look up; too much to be done.

Internally, I was warmed by the reception for me, especially from women, people of color, and very specifically from Black employees. I was surprised at the early meetings and conversations so many women wanted to have, about everything from desiring family-friendly benefits to challenging cultures within various engineering groups. Mostly, though, people just wanted to say "We are so happy you are in this role." It took me a while to realize their emphasis on "*you*." They recognized me as someone noted for seeing and valuing people.

Externally, the story was not the one I anticipated. My "firstness" was of huge significance. There were congratulatory letters and notes from around the world, from various type of organizations, some discreetly attempting to secure a place of favor, because this is what people do. But there were also notes and letters from the most unexpected places, especially from my community. *My* community was proud. I heard from the president of Grambling State University, and the Supreme Basileus (president) of my sorority, Alpha Kappa Alpha, wrote to me directly. Black organizations, churches, schools, and Black people wrote to me. They called. Sent flowers, cards. The ELC—the only Black networking organization composed of C-level Black executives—sent me congratulations. Diane Abbott, the only Black female member of Parliament in the UK, sent me a note of congratulations. I'd met her years before and had invited her and her son, James, to the Regent Street Apple Store opening in London. I was also followed, even stalked, by job seekers, smiled at constantly by favor seekers, and pitched to consistently by pretty much anyone who envisioned their dreams to be in perfect concert with Apple's mission.

I had a vision for my new role, and the accumulated insight to know there was much more to do and more impact to make. I wanted to establish a new talent relationship for Apple, new partnerships with communities where tech was severely underrepresented. I held hope for a more connected, more welcoming culture that incorporated the existing attributes that made Apple a great innovator. I firmly believed the company could be made better and richer by embracing empathy, and through the cultivation of even more talented people who saw and valued humanity as central to their purpose.

I reached out to a couple of confidants, asking for their insight and sharing that I was focused on how I would assemble a team and get work moving. They affirmed my thinking but added an element that had eluded me. One of my closest friends, a media exec, put it this way: "You are in rooms with some of the top leaders in the world, making the most popular products in the world. You are privy to a lauded and famously secretive company's most confidential information. You are responsible for the top talent in the world. You have influence most people can't remotely fathom. And you are a woman and you are Black. Understand this, then keep it moving. But do not fail to understand its significance."

That was why all the hoopla. People are promoted all the time, for Pete's sake, but I could not dismiss the ancestral understanding of what had transpired nor dismiss its importance. I also could not expect those who did not *see* to understand the significance. But I did ultimately register the complexity of it all. As much as the move was taken in stride by other colleagues and leaders, as they simply expected me to do my job, it was the unspoken parts of what I represented that I felt responsibility and accountability to. It mattered. I mattered.

There is an ever-present fact within the Black community that when someone reaches a notable height, we also brace for the blowback. We support and exhort so enthusiastically because we anticipate what follows. Finally, I got that, felt it. I embraced what this all represented, then quickly just dug in. I dove into things while placing a temporary psychological hold on my plans to depart for the life I had been shaping. I knew there was unfinished business: challenges around diversity, culture, communication, and empathy, as well as the fundamental leading of a global operation. The latter part I knew I could do; I had done it. I never doubted my capability; I doubted whether I was seeing my own soul's desire.

Whenever those doubts surfaced, I turned to the music—the songs I'd loved for the bulk of my life. Verdi's and Puccini's stories of heroines of class and caste. The laments of life, love, and funk from Motown and Philly; the wails of Chaka, the respect of Aretha, the trills of Kathleen, and the reigning ovation of Leontyne, as the African princess Aida. Ella's and

Sarah's sheer elegance. I called upon them all to move me along, as theirs were the stories I knew, and in those stories I could believe in an outcome where I could see myself survive, possibly even thrive?

I used whatever spare time I carved out during this time to record my own stories, my own music. Holding no expectation of the music being commercially viable, that made it thrilling to make. I could just create art: tell stories, collaborate with talented artists, and evoke emotion that convinced people it really was okay to feel. This was a life-affirming diversion from my corporate life, and I relished it.

Chapter 14

Not a Passion Project

Not to know is bad, not to want to know is worse.

—GAMBIAN PROVERB

As HR chief, it had become my responsibility to lay the foundation of Apple's diversity position publicly. But more important, to do so with our own employees, a conversation yet to be had. I launched and implemented some overdue policies and practices, such as extended family leave and general paid leaves. We created the first public accountability report on demographics and progress; I brokered what was at that time the largest corporate contribution to date to HBCUs through the TMCF; we strengthened relationships with the organizations that knew how to support women in technology, NCWIT and The Grace Hopper Program; we pushed for enhanced benefits for women and families; and my team drove gender pay equity globally. This was all great work, but oh-so-basic and not yet even remotely unpacking the deeper challenges to an inclusive ecosystem.

The whole conversation on equity was still a new conversation, and one still met with significant resistance across tech companies, known for a "meritocritous" philosophy. Most executives made room in their minds for diversity in the areas of recruiting and demographics but had little sense of the depth of impact systemic inequity and injustice had on their own employees and teams. For years, the breakdown of education and other social systems were blamed. But the role commerce could play, and specifically technology, was simply not grasped.

Internally, companies grappled with how much was "fair" to spend with diverse contractors, vendors, advertisers, suppliers, developers—all the infrastructure that upheld the company. It was profoundly missed by most companies that this was a systemic fissure they could positively impact. Instead, small diverse businesses were asked to jump higher and farther to prove their worth. This dearth of insight was the real test of a company's pledges and commitments. And for those of us carrying the flags for the work it all felt a bit like using a wooden pick to prick a breathing hole in a zeppelin.

Dr. John Powell, who heads the UC Berkeley Othering and Belonging Institute (formerly the Haas Institute for a Fair and Inclusive Society), was a mentor and one of my most important teachers in the work of race, equity, inclusion, and belonging. Like myself, Dr. Powell eschewed the tossing about of corporate buzzwords, jargon, and acronyms. He focused instead on the pure and universally understood concept of "belonging," supported by neuroscience; how the brain and the subconscious works within all of us. He didn't try to "solve for" solutions; he knew the work required what it required, and he also seemed to instinctively know how few would endeavor it.

From Stanford professor Claude Steele's "stereotype threat," when our minds fill in blanks with biased information, to the well-known research finding that résumés with Black-sounding names secure fewer interviews than those with white-sounding names, and many more, the session Dr. Powell offered us introduced a solid balance of new thinking alongside what most people believed they already knew. If thinking people sat in his sessions, you left with more insight and an unresolved sense of "why" that just might spur you to want to read and understand more.

Dr. Powell's noted work on belonging was about human interaction and how we each create the conditions that signal to others whether they belong or not. John's concept of how belonging manifested did not play as a "soft "concept but addressed the science of why it is biologically essential that we thrive as human beings. That belonging means more than just having access; it means having a meaningful voice and the opportunity to participate. He'd trained federal judges, Hollywood scriptwriters, emergency room nurses, and many more on how to identify bias, and create belonging that led to thriving. His work resonated for me, as it represented an intelligent mixture of business thinking with human-centered practices, much of what we had done for years inside of Apple Stores. His work made it ever-more clear why training programs, proclamations, reports, hiring metrics, and inclusion pledges gleaned minimal results. His presentation did not shy away from the realities of social injustices and systemic inequities, but it did offer that there was a path to *better* that we all could contribute toward. In his pilot sessions he did acknowledge that there was difficult, humanly honest work involved in creating belonging. It was work most companies didn't know they needed to do and thus did not even start to consider until the summer of 2020. Before that moment in time, the need for a different and deeper level of effort was still being dismissed or denied, and the practitioners of diversity were still being blamed for the full enterprise failure at being diverse, which was, in reality, failure at creating a thriving culture. John's work felt honest, integral, and important to the conversations we hoped lie ahead.

My team knew well how much our leaders needed this material. We also knew well that our leaders were at varying points along an awareness continuum. We knew well we'd be met with an array of responses from "I need this data to be further proven" to "I already know this so how do we solve it, let's get it fixed." We held hope that Dr. Powell's approach, and the fact that the existing narrative was not making a dent in representation, would offer a needed boost. This was in the thick of the "lack of representation in tech" conversations, and only a glimpse of time before *diversity* became the politically and culturally charged term it is today.

I held the hope that this was the right time to help my colleagues see and understand the depth of our diversity issues and the possibilities to be gleaned if we really committed to a new way of seeing the issues, and if we were to push beyond trite numerical outcomes. So I brought in John Powell, law professor, revered academic, world-renowned expert, to talk to the key leaders in the company about the concept of a culture of belonging, a concept for which he was considered a global expert. He'd address community, thriving, systemic and historic inequity, the science of bias, the power of culture. He would pilot his session, then work with us to develop our version of it to deliver broadly.

I believed it could move us past a check-the-box approach. I envisioned we could even start to think about using our own technology to propagate a new and better awareness of the lexicon on belonging, enabling the breadth and depth of Apple's platforms to drive new ways of interacting with and embracing others. The prescience of using Apple technology to facilitate belonging proved later to be even more ironic, as it was an iPhone 11 used by Darnella Frazier to capture the murder of George Floyd, arguably the most important civil rights film of a generation.

One might want to think it would be simple for the chief HR executive for a global tech organization to bring in one of the most sought-after academics on the topic of inclusion and belonging, but as a Black woman, I knew I had to be thoughtful and strategic about who spoke to the company's top leaders on this topic. All diversity practitioners will recognize this angst. Who, what, and how anything is deemed credible is always a dicey proposition, and in this case particularly so, because underlying the discussion was great sensitivity around race, access, privilege, equity, and injustice. Topics intrinsically familiar to most people of color, but topics that represented significant discomfort for those in power.

Dr. Powell came with his research assistant, Dr. Vicky Plaut, a Hispanic woman, so a Black and brown slate of presenters would be speaking to mostly white, minimally female leadership teams from various parts of the company. We could very easily be met with polite smiles, nods, frequent iPhone checks, and a few actual departures from the meeting, dripping with "Sorry, I've gotta run, got a conflict" or "I was just called upstairs, please fill me in later." The kind of meetings I'd hoped for would find my colleagues enlightened, asking questions, abandoning discomfort or denial quickly, and allowing Dr. Powell to lead them into discovery. That was my hope. Yet, I knew that in tech and many engineering cultures anything presented is subject to debate. And most concerning to me, and despite what might be claimed, I knew that because John Powell was a Black man, what he said would be dissected and scrutinized, consciously and subconsciously. I fretted about whether he'd be seen and heard properly. How would he dress? How would his age and demeanor be processed? John is a tall, elegant, stately, steely-haired, at the time sixty-eight-year-old man, who speaks softly and deliberately, and not at the rapid clip and cadence known to be standard tech speak. I needed to assess all possible outcomes to try to ensure that John himself would not sense exclusion as he stood to inform *us* about exclusion. I also knew there would be deniers of my concerns. "You don't have to do all of that thinking for us," someone would invariably assert. And as I had learned over years of being a Black woman, the most ardent deniers are always the perpetrators. Oh, the irony.

But I didn't let my angst distract my focus. I knew that if John could get through to even one or two from the targeted audiences it would make a tremendous difference. These were brilliant, influential people; surely some would take away what we hoped they would. These tenets of inclusion had not been wholly embraced at the senior-most levels at Apple since the late-nineties years of Santiago Rodriguez, who long predated the current executive leaders. But I believed we could get there. The whole point of most of John's research was that people are not conscious of their subconscious levels of scrutiny, but John and I and every other person of color know unconscious scrutiny intimately. Even more important, the tenets of John's work were scientific, asserting that all of our brains categorize according to our cultural cues, and the socialization we all receive determines our actions, which meant our actions were correctable with awareness. These were minds who could grasp this, or so I hoped.

John and I talked through basic speaker protocol for folks coming into Apple: convincingly using Apple products for one's presentation, balancing being casually dressed with professionally represented, and so on. We smiled about his gray hair, his towering height. All unique human traits no one would think twice about, except that we were talking about a subject that made people uncomfortable, afraid, defensive, and likely to attack the messenger for the content being somehow inadequate, and the messenger overly invested, too biased "in reverse," somehow less credible.

My team shared my angst from their own experiences, and we worked over John's keynote presentation multiple times, leading with the neuroscience, facts, and stats before getting into the areas of potential debate and discomfort. John and his team were not paid much for these early visits, yet worked as hard to prepare as when they were welcomed with open arms and checkbooks by other major organizations. This kind of meta work that diversity practitioners and/or people of color often do is a distant cousin to the "we have to work twice as hard" adage. It is, in translation, *when we are in positions of power or influence, we have to work harder to set others up to be heard and accepted by our powerful peers.*

In the end, Dr. Powell presented to several leadership teams, more than half of the participants we'd aimed for. Publicly, there was favorable feedback. Some even enthusiastically thanked us for the more enlightening aspects of his presentation. I knew there was a quieter narrative circulating, but I was not privy to it. And as is the norm with most companies' diversity office budgets, funding was always tentative. My budget for this work was modest, so if large-scale work was to be done, senior leaders needed to help fund it, and they'd do so only if they believed it would "fix the diversity numbers," which was the sole motivating objective.

Dr. Powell asked the attendees of his sessions for more personal self-reflection and unlearning of old beliefs, and to take initiative to learn more about themselves. He described an inclusive culture, not media-published metrics, as the true arbiter of DEI success. He used the term "belonging," and when he did, I watched faces in the room go blank or bodies squirm. It was as if they were asked to—but avoided—reaching back into their lives to a time when they felt they belonged, were truly a part of something. This required remembering, revisiting, reassessing. It meant using a different language, a different part of the brain. It meant being uncomfortably honest about beliefs that had been overtly taught or subconsciously accepted. It may have meant realizing that by not speaking up or acting against something they really had been condoning it. This required feeling. It was not a matter of rightness nor wrongness. It meant empathizing with someone else's experience, seeing how it was valid. It meant seeing.

I suppose I was disappointed at the lukewarm reception to this level of effort, but not surprised. These were the same creators, the brilliant, problem-solving, world-changing minds I'd worked with for years. And although a few privately said to me "I know this is the right work to be doing," it still lost the popular vote, the one that would be reported to our shared boss.

Despite how compelling John was to quite a few leaders, it was the term "belonging" that failed to get traction. In post debriefs, I was advised not to use it, to stick with "hard metrics" that execs could "relate to." Sigh . . . Numbers, 1; Humanity, 0. Humanity backed with numbers, maybe a 2. I realized I'd watched rooms full of smart people revert to a comfort zone, the same comfort zone that had secured us minimal traction for increasing representation, and less than minimal progress at creating a richer experience for the "numbers" of us that lived and worked each day. The mandate, my mandate as HR chief, was simply to "fix diversity." I suppose this is because what engineers do is fix, and my teams and I would need to continue the effort of reframing what "fixing" really meant. I watched my team move on in efforts to distract themselves from absorbing this as an ongoing failure narrative. What we did instead was focus on enriching the culture for employees by putting their all into meaningful events, prominent speakers, attending to incoming interns, creating content and programs. Because I ran a full global HR function, we ran our business of managing talent and culture. But we all knew this was not the real work, just as all practitioners of HR, culture, DEI, Learning and Development understand this, and that the real issues were not being unearthed.

I knew from my life experiences, and years of studying humans, that most people are not ready to do the work required to see themselves, and especially not something as serious as how we all perpetuate systems of oppression and inequity. What companies want is a solution that integrates comfortably, that is quantitative and moves numbers, no matter how shallow the footprint of that movement. That is never going to be the solution, but we can keep talking about it for a few more decades.

I attended a conference in downtown San Francisco on workplace diversity, sponsored by Mercer (a premier HR services company) and was both impressed and dismayed by the attendees, who were mostly heads of HR or a newly created "diversity" role. Talented, smart, mostly women and women of color, they lamented and relayed scenarios that the respective heads of their companies should have been embarrassed by. As experts and professionals, meetings with their executives were often delegated to a non–decision making stand-in, receiving lower and lower prioritization. These DEI folks waxed brutally honest, as they spoke of being put on the "spot" in presentations to "prove" why diversity worked when they were "already successful." They were confronted with the "quota debate," insisting any diversity goals were quotas, the lowering of standards, and grounds for a general wringing of hands. There was outright rudeness, dismissiveness, and of course, as always, there was the almost-professionally-abusive use of funding, then defunding. There were hiring "freezes" as soon as more than a few people of color had been brought in. The stories and laments from this room full of professionals could have gone for hours, and the conference—designed to share best practices with a highly regarded organization like Mercer—instead became a cathartic haven for defeated and disillusioned practitioners. I sat in the conference sinking in spirit, observing a room full of talent being wasted. I also realized at some level that they were being exposed to workplace trauma. As dramatic as that sounds, the realness of it—exposure to untenable, unsustainable conditions, constantly shifting assessments, new barriers, old biases—it was a battle they all knew was not winnable yet they suited up because they remained optimistic . . . or because they needed jobs, likely both. It was one of the saddest experiences I'd recalled in years. I was silently thankful my journey had seen a broader, fuller dimension of my positive impact during my time at

Apple because this work decidedly would not be seen with the same lens of success.

It is fascinating to think that companies place the responsibility for creating a culture of belonging into the hands of one person: one DRI (directly responsible individual). No other large-scale initiative requiring a business systems management would be so minimally supported. But the work of culture and thriving is still profoundly misunderstood and holds an inherently biased place in the minds of decision-makers. It is still, for some of the most successful executives in the land, a soft and mysterious practice, this idea of cultivating how human beings can thrive.

I recall having a meeting on team selection and challenges with diverse hiring with a respected top technology executive. We had a reasonable conversation. I say reasonable, although I did most of the talking and he did more head nodding. Toward the end of the meeting he said, "It's so great you're doing this work—this is such a passion for you." What work? A passion for *me*?

Had this been one of those clever movie outtakes, here's what I would have said to him in my total Black chick tone: "No, this is my job, to mirror back to *you* how *you* are the one who owns the successful outcome here. It is *your* work to be done, *your* managers that must produce, learn, and unlearn. This is not *my* passion project, I am here to advise *you,* and I am damn good at it. The 'passion' you feel is the heat of *my* excellence, and my pent-up impatience for why we are still having these damn conversations. You are as accountable for the outcomes of this work as I am, so please do not treat this as my *problem,* my *passion,* or my *charitable work.*"

Ah, then the camera would reset to the real conversation,

the one where I knew that he in no way understood what he had just said or the extent to which it annoyed me. I knew this and had to decide what to say in that moment, caught between the cluelessness of this highly regarded executive and my sheer exasperation. Without realizing it, a C-level leader had demonstrated precisely why tech was late to the acknowledgment of its responsibility. He had just outsourced humanity, inclusion, and culture to me, but unlike the many years when I thought something was mine because they said it was, this time I was unwilling to receive it. Just like the lovely diversity leaders at the conference I'd attended, I too had the bucket handed back to me as my passion work. Leaders who'd not learned the preeminence of their role in the human side of leadership. Leaders for whom building a representative, creative, healthy, and belonging culture was someone else's job. Significant leaders with the ability to make decisions that could shift a narrative of a generation of corporate cultures. Leaders whom no one had the courage to tell otherwise (often including myself), whose personas were tired and exhausting for their employees. Leaders who had no understanding of a different kind of power versus the perceived "power" they'd been acclimated to garnering throughout their careers and lives. I recall in that moment reaching a place where I knew I could no longer restrain myself, and when, not if, it came up in a next conversation it would yield very differently. Fortunately, I recall the next conversation was with Jony Ive, and it was, as always, an entirely different experience, enriched with kindness, thoughtfulness, wit, ideas, and as always, running long over our allotted time. Jony had given me a reprieve where I could tap into our shared creative essence, and I doubt he ever realized how he'd salvaged that day for me.

The frustration from that meeting and the similar ones that had happened over the years is the song sung by diversity pros. And just when we're making headway, the usual suspects of race, class, and systemically biased corporate thinking are tossed like a grenade into a conversation: "We can't lower our standards," "I need to avoid hiring risks," "We need someone to hit the ground running right now," and "I can see her ready for leadership in a few years," among too many others. These and other common diversity-opposed phrases set conversations and people into a backward spin. There is rarely opportunity to educate as to why this language and these discussions are fraught with inequity, bias, sexism, racism, and ultimately, harm. I wish more leaders knew that in their lack of ownership for increasing their cultural competence, they lose the respect of their people. And when you are not respected, you are not believed.

Within this same accountability vacuum, too many diversity practitioners internalize failure. They think, *I must not have done a good enough job messaging or presenting the work.* They work harder to develop a message they believe leadership will find more palatable and embrace. But when leadership has no motivation to do the hard work of self-examination, unlearning, and relearning, there will be no consciousness shift to support an already difficult cultural shift. Diversity practitioners catch the greasy slick balls constantly tossed at them, then try to hold on to them and make themselves game ready. It's exhausting, and it leaves dedicated people feeling unsuccessful, unheard, and unseen.

That, in part, is why I eschewed roles whose title contained "diversity" or other configurations of the DEI acronym. I believed the title was a lightning rod for deflection. For the entirety of my work life, especially in HR and culture leadership, I have always done the work the diversity title warrants, because it was critical to my role. Words matter, and people have traditionally not handled well this set of charged words we have strung together: diversity, inclusion, equity. I say this with infinite respect for my fellow practitioners of diversity; for all that is right and just about it, their hard work and commitment has undoubtedly made profound impact in this world. But it should have been exponentially more.

I have long believed that the CEO should actually hold the title of Chief Diversity Officer—not that person of color who shoulders the tidal wave of human biases and beliefs, and faces down insurmountable obstacles neither seen nor understood by the NPOC (non–people of color, in the spirit of using acronyms).

The "diversity officer" is expected to enact change where an invisible, systemic, and ingrained set of beliefs works against their every move. And if a DO launches a plan to seriously address the human issues this work entails, they can count on a limited tenure in their role. They represent discomfort, their methodology is rarely understood, and they are all too frequently deemed an expense rather than an investment. Either they read the tea leaves for themselves, or it is decided in a room where they are not present that "We are just not ready to prioritize this" or "We just don't see the needle moving" or other such nonsensical assertions. This diversity officer type role can expect a short shelf life.

Another way companies execute DEI leadership is to spend time creating an abundance of metrics on activities held—events, conferences, programs—maybe even numbers hired and interns. Perhaps even create an impressive marketing campaign and run it often. But absent is a shared language, competence in building human connection, education on historical context, and tools for having today the kind of conversations that were never allowed in workplaces. The idea of building skills and environments that help people see and hear one another makes CFOs and CEOs sharpen their red pencils. And for teams of diversity pros across the nation these remain unfulfilling jobs, tied to empty metrics for show and tell.

When it appeared for me, I already had lots of data. In early 2017 I knew I was headed for the very thing I had sidestepped my entire career. Tim asked me to take on the role (or label, as it felt to me) of vice president of inclusion and diversity. Again, even as my internal voice of reason and sanity said no, I said yes to a company I still believed capable of doing this differently, better, smarter, as they'd done so many other times. The call for tech companies to step up to address their abysmal lack of representation in race and gender had reached a fever pitch. I saw the need to keep the conversation moving; I thought having it was a healthy sign of change. I had worked my entire career to help people be seen; now I saw a way to do more of it and with systemic impact and the broader support I was assured.

I also seriously considered the role because I had both a clear vision and an end game in mind, wanting this work shifted from the trite narrative of numbers, programs, and pipeline to expanding the thinking around representation into products, imagery, messaging, places where Apple was already successful. I wanted to make sure we understood that DEI was as critical to how we interacted with customers and stakeholders, creating a culture of inclusion for them as well. And finally, I thought again of my dad, who many decades earlier reluctantly took the helm of leadership as a "first" in the city of Colorado Springs—a first city councilman in his district, a first vice mayor, and a first African American to serve as mayor. I recalled a segment of his obituary that I must have internalized. It read, "Young, who died last week at age 80, championed equal treatment and opportunity for city employees; fought to improve neighborhoods; and supported the acquisition of water supplies and construction of a new airport, which helped position the city for today's growth." His era's version of diversity, equity, access, inclusion, and seeing. I had his imprint. My thinking was to push on the qualitative first—connecting authentically, not artificially, to people of color, to people who frequently felt excluded, to people—including our *employees*—who felt unseen. I knew that connecting at that human level would ultimately show quantitative results. When people feel seen, they activate, they engage, they invite others to share the experience, they feel safer to give of themselves, to contribute ideas, even to work harder. These are outcomes that absolutely can be measured. But not without first doing the human work.

In my earnestness to establish a new lens for DEI, I did not recognize at the time just how much my use of words from a more empathic and communal-based lexicon did not resonate with executive thinking. I knew, of course, it was a different way to frame the challenge, and I believed it to be the way headway would be made. I reported to a CEO who, given his life experiences, I believed to be much further along the awareness continuum. I had a short list of leaders I knew who strongly resonated with this lens, even if they would not admit it publicly. Those who'd historically wanted measured and rationalized metrics I also prioritized to tag them for reframing conversations. I had a good starting plan.

． ． ．

Over the years I'd worked often with the renowned competency expert Bob Eichinger, introduced to me by one of his former students. I vividly recalled how when I was first promoted to Apple's HR chief, Bob reached out to congratulate me, but with a warning: "I have always thought you to be a brilliant and thoughtful leader, but you must remember you do not speak the same language as your new boss. Be careful; you may not be on the same page most of the time." This prediction did have some merit, but not in the ways I think Bob believed it would.

From Tim and my peers, I was given space to be the voice for people and human decisions and the voice they relied on to speak on areas they might miss. This I did. Bob's warning, however, was indeed borne out, and it had just manifested in this new role. The gap between how I saw an executive job leading diversity and how the CEO saw it was the same gap dilemma many DEI leaders faced and still face. Many years prior, in the late nineties, I had heard from Apple's first employee tasked with diversity work; a visionary, and his insight resonated in ways I still viscerally remembered. I had the benefit of this teaching, and several decades of experiences to pull from. I'd studied with a Berkeley professor on the topic. Yet I knew, from living that same journey of experiences, that what was now being asked for in this role was not achievable. I had another view of a pathway to achieving it. And that was the most apparent manifestation of different languages at play that a renowned leadership expert had predicted.

As I stepped, somewhat reluctantly yet still hopefully, into a role with an industry history of failure, I called Bob again.

"I absolutely would not do it," he said.

I sighed, simultaneously wrestling to rationalize my reasons against his advice, but also with my own inner caution light flashing. Bob was a seventies white-male-leadership guru who had trained mostly white males for decades. Why was I even asking him? Because Bob was someone who intimately knew the system I would face in this role, and he did not see me winning, changing, or even putting a dent in it. I wanted to at least know the odds of the reality ahead.

So, to use my music background metaphorically, as the corporate chorus singing the "diversity is important" theme grew louder and more frantic, I conceded to the volume but didn't heed the meaning of the song, didn't study the text or the composer. I did negotiate with myself, and I vowed that once I'd made some sort of headway I could reactivate my plans to leave corporate life, follow my dad's guidance from years prior, hopefully with my spirit intact enough to move into my next phase. I had been at the company for twenty-plus years and risen to the top under two famous CEOs. Now I was wearying of not listening to my creative life's voice, the one that had been calling me but I kept putting on hold.

Once again, the media wrote about me as a historical "first," with the inclusion and diversity title I never loved on others or for myself. The media emphasized how Apple had never had this role at a C-suite level, that it was a big commitment, and a hopeful one, given my track record with the company. Meantime, at least three professional colleagues in other industry sectors called me and said, "Run for the hills! You have been great. Do not do this. Is it too late to refuse?"

I sighed.

As my proof of concept, gender, orientation, and accessibility had already been accepted and embraced as diversity priorities; in fact, Apple's products had been leading in accessibility for decades. But real conversation on racial and cultural biases, systemic inequities, and how it all permeated the company's behaviors? This was all new, and a much heavier lift. We had no language for having these conversations, and any shared understanding of the issues and their root cause would be a challenge to say the least. Whisperings from Black employees expressed the typical conundrum of weariness with translating and explaining when their challenges came into the workplace, which they did. In the wake of the disproportionate incidents of violent and fatal police encounters, Black employees wanted to feel safe and hear from us that we cared about their safe coming and going. A new administration that made immigrants, Dreamers, military veterans, and more feel breathtakingly othered, employees wanted to hear more, and the conversations came up regardless of the company's readiness to have them. This work presented itself as an even bigger challenge because the same qualities that had produced the most admired products in the world—narrowed focus, a clinical obsession for detail, exclusivity, secrecy, privacy—were not the qualities that would nurture or embrace an inclusive and belonging culture. The elements of emotional intelligence needed to be interwoven into an already tightly knit fabric.

Internally, Apple University worked with me on the challenge, addressing the identification and individualism of diversity. It was intelligent work, but it was not the work that would penetrate the invisible, unspoken monolith we now faced. What was now needed was a way to connect human to human, so that new conversations on how race, racial inequity, biases, and the stronghold of a white-male-centric culture manifested itself so pervasively in corporate America, and in the hearts and minds of Americans.

I felt the most alone I have felt in my entire career, as I attempted to find a language strong and powerful enough to name and address issues but not bludgeon the predominantly male and white leadership that surrounded me, which would render the effort fini before I could begin. Black professionals know the blowback, denial, and indignation that arises from even remotely suggesting that a white colleague may hold human biases, have had privileges, or benefited from systems not accessible to historically marginalized people. Prior to 2020, we as Black professionals did what we could to avoid that face-off, we knew it all too well, and it was rarely worth the fire and smoke it generated. We had lives to live; people were tired.

To address this same leadership elite who'd made technology history, who'd soon become the first trillion-dollar technology company, who'd repeatedly changed the world in countless ways and industries, there was in those moments only me and a small handful of brave appointees attempting the heavy lifting of these conversations. I felt like the soloist asserting a cadenza of how we and our products could be made even better to an audience that did not understand why exactly I was even singing.

They were not making the connection, but not disagreeing. There was enthusiastic agreement and some vigorous nodding as I presented my intentions, but I knew from each conversation that they were not seeing themselves as crucial to the equation, not seeing the powerful and compelling ways *they*—and *only* they—could make the changes that would move us forward.

As my diversity colleagues in tech companies frequently

put it, DEI became our bug to fix, but with no access to design, code, flow, resources. Even if we could gain access to these elements, we were facing down an engineering failure due to lack of understanding of the problem. The owner of the problem was now me, and as DEI folks across the world know, this kind of ownership does not translate in the way a product launch or software release is owned. For these, entire teams of people hold responsibility and accountability. When they are thanked at big tech company product launches, there are "too many teams and names to mention," and apologies are rendered for any omission.

What happens with a perceived diversity failure? We are named by name, the way our mothers used to call us in for supper. I know many of my tech colleagues shared in this experience, but I felt especially frustrated and profoundly alone in my attempts to help us to see ourselves. My smart, often prescient, wildly successful company was not seeing what the world expected us to see so clearly.

I watched and admired as my colleague and friend Lisa Jackson gained considerable traction in shifting the company toward environmental responsibility. Lisa is brilliant and certainly faced down the barriers and challenges inherent to her field, and yes, also to her presenting as a Black woman. However, I often wondered if there was any advantage to leading work that sat in the tech comfort zones of science and engineering, while I grappled with the land mines in the fields of race, gender, culture, belief systems, and layers of messy human complexity.

As much as my role or that of any diversity officer may be evidence of a company's intent to do the right work, nevertheless each day, every conversation turns into, to varying degrees, a debate over worthiness, efficacy, and cost. DEI practitioners are expected to match or mirror business practices that will fit this work onto spreadsheets, within budget timelines. Did anyone really understand the issues at play here? Did no one see why for years there had been no movement or traction in diverse representation? Where was the problem-solving, world-changing, innovating, seeing-around-corners zeitgeist the world was looking to technology for? Or were all of us in DEI correct in translating the incoming messages as "You, diversity departments everywhere, need to make this work for us, without our having to intellectually, logically, emotionally, or psychologically invest in understanding why it has never worked before. That had to be due to circumstances beyond our reach, like poor school systems, broken families, and urban decay. If we don't get it, just train us to get it. Then show us diverse people who fit our standards, our policies, and protocols. Tell us what to do to fix diversity and the media narrative, while you find great people for us, bring them in, and make sure they interview well and stand tall above all other candidates, because of course we don't want to lower our standards when we already have people we can hire: our friends, neighbors, kids of friends, and friends of friends."

This is the unspoken response to diversity efforts that no one wants to admit to, and it is the dilemma of representation in technology and beyond. It is what DEI teams still face daily. Rarely have leaders connected the holistic story of cultural and racial economics, the systematic disenfranchisement that is core to America, directly to the issues of representation within their walls. For years, these were conversations considered to be too uncomfortable, too broad, even futile; after all, "that was the past and so long ago" and surely there are roads to being more diverse, we just need to find the "right" people to map them out for us.

Then in 2020, the George Floyd murder raised the conversation to a fevered pitch with mainstream America everywhere. Called a moment of "reckoning," it was not that for us, for we had been forced to "reckon" with years of it. This moment of public exposure of who we are as a society finally broke through the comfort barrier. The veneer of acceptable ignorance had been breached. This moment happened, and as much as we hoped otherwise, what swiftly followed was social and political polarization, giving way to the inevitable backlash, denials, and attempts to rewrite or restate what we all saw with raw vision.

We had a moment, a moment that we all know changed the course of the planet. Whether acknowledged or not, May 25, 2020, changed every one of our lives. But the subsequent pullback that followed it offered organizations a way of sheltering themselves from hard talk, and ultimately even harder actions. It requires professional and personal courage to understand and address the challenges of DEI work in any industry. It takes developing new communication skills, most of all from top organizational leaders, something simply not part of the mandate to produce shareholder value, and still hardly taught in traditional business school programs. What happened in the summer of 2020 was a horror that was a mirror of us, not an isolated disaster. It gave permission for everyone to be deeply, humanly horrified, even if we'd seen the scenes before. Yet for all but the direct witnesses, too many saw it from a distance, as if wearing far-sighted readers, then removing them and placing them on the nightstand.

I tried to avoid the title of chief diversity officer until I didn't. I somehow knew I had to face it down and to better understand it for the sake of the others I might help. Help to the CDOs I frequently counsel, help to the CEOs asking the how-to-do-this questions or the HR departments grappling with the ever-present demand for DEI efficacy without commitment. To them all, I say this: It is the hardest work in your organization. Every day, people in your charge with "diversity" attached to their names are coming up against walls of resistance and indifference, language barriers, personal and political belief barriers, denial, dismissiveness, and flat-out backlash. They are facing down key leaders at every single level of an organization who possess minimal awareness and generally a shallow understanding of what diversity work is, or why it has to be done. In today's world, the politics of the country and world are primed and set to litigate the very existence of anything "diversity" related. Yet fundamental common sense tells us it is more critical than ever to address, and to address authentically, empathetically, and humbly.

To any CEO reading this: If you want to prepare the ground for the culture shift required to do real work in DEI, then consider the following and much more. Treat your DEI officers and teams the way you treat and engage with your most valued people, doing the most valued work, the work that generates the most return for your organization. Signal their value to the entire company by how you treat them. Do not delegate them to another executive, especially not to your human resources or social responsibility leader, where they can be categorized, and incorrectly so. This work should always directly report to you. If you don't have bandwidth for it, either make it, or don't do it.

Start with you. Take an honest inventory of what you believe and the origin of those beliefs. You don't have to change them, but you do need to know more about the layers of beliefs that inform your decisions. Over time you may or may not evolve your thinking or beliefs and you may resist learning or unlearning. But the same voracious absorption you apply to learn about marketplace complexity—which your shareholders rely upon you to do—is required by this work and deserves the same energy. It is no different; you should have working competence and staff experts advising you.

As you would in the marketplace, educate yourself and come to the table knowing more about the challenges your DEI team faces, so you'll be able to help problem-solve more effectively. This is what you would do in the face of engineering or operations. Get to know who your DEI team is. Engage, make real connection, listen carefully, see them. Ask the kinds of questions you would ask of your most valued leaders. Treat their subject matter with the same genuine interest and concern you do with the people representing the work that your company most relies on. At the end of the day, it turns out that it is as critically important.

Make your diversity, inclusion, and equity leaders a part of your inner circles. Everyone around you already knows who or what you care most about, even whom you most enjoy spending time around. Make certain that DEI budgets remain available and robust. Do not burden them unnecessarily with credentialing and "best practices," because this work truly has not yet seen its best practices. Only in rare organizations with rare leaders has it been given sufficient time and the longitudinal support to demonstrate efficacy.

Don't impose metrics on this team that don't apply to real

change or real movement. They will respect you for resisting the executive urge to issue busywork metrics that say nothing authentic or meaningful about real human beings. It is important to measure, but work to establish metrics of impact: what engages, enriches, and why, and the metrics of thriving, all of which will translate to better, more thoughtful products or services. We understand that the words and measurements that describe how human beings move, feel, and behave are different from the measures of financial growth, yet we use the same underlying principles that x=y and y=thriving.

Don't shy away from the stories of human impact. Framing this work with the art of storytelling is powerful, especially as told by the top leaders in the organization. Your authentic stories hold incredible power. People listen to and act on your words. Don't be afraid of this idea, which is what is meant by "leading." Don't be fearful of being deemed "soft" or "anecdotal"; these words are deployed when things make us humanly uncomfortable. You, the topmost leaders of the business world and the world at large, are the very ones we all need to hear being softer, and more personal, less scripted. Allowing yourself to be seen is a power flex of the twenty-first century. It is very much a show of power, and power for good.

Last, do untested, uncomfortable things that help people. Mandate more positive impact value simply because you can. Not everything has to be rehearsed, tested, and tried. You are paid millions for the great instincts we know you have, so use them. You *can* meet an HBCU engineering dean on your campus or building and ask them on the spot to help you recruit talent. You *can* ask your executives to read Isabel Wilkerson's book *Caste: The Origins of Our Discontent*. You *can* insist that staff within a certain radius of or planning a business trip to Washington, DC, visit the National Museum of African American History and Culture. You can insist that English-only mandates be relaxed, then realize suddenly that you're oozing with new talent in areas critical to supporting your business. You can do more. So much more.

If these adjustments seem obvious to you as a leader, or you believe you're already making them, you probably sit atop a culture primed to embrace thriving as a measurement of success. If you lead a public company, you have very likely already primed your shareholders and your board that this is the direction to take, as Tim Cook once energetically did in an Apple shareholders meeting, or as BlackRock's Larry Fink once did when he wrote personal letters to all his executives about the criticality of diverse hiring. If you believe you've done much of this and you still aren't getting traction, consider that more time may be needed. Often, it's a matter of how the work is talked about. Leaders don't like to talk about things "unless there is progress," progress defined in nonimpact, quantitative, "how many" kinds of ways. Progress can be compelling when we tell stories about it. Progress is believed when it is honest, authentic, and genuinely committed to.

If you believe your efforts are not influencing movement, then pause, reflect, and investigate the reasons why, with the same concern and fervor you would bring to a product or service concern. Have the same determination to win, to succeed in human work, and believe it is what is expected of you. Try to understand this is a different world, a world that needs you to behave differently. And if you simply can't invest in this counsel, then you likely should not. But I'd debate you in any forum that you should be doing "human" work if humans are who your organization employs! And I would urge you to list all the ways your organization would suffer if attention to the human condition is not strategically and intentionally planned for.

A CEO I know well spoke at one of my board meetings on how he was rethinking his company's commitment to diversity. He attributed the shift in thinking to the litany of violent incidents befalling young African American men, women and boys, and, ultimately, the tragedies of the summer of 2020. He related that his daughters had called him out intently on his prior stances. Their words shook him, and as a result he took a step back to reflect on his own belief systems. He read books. He asked questions. He took risks, both personal and professional, as he had no idea how his own team would respond to this level of energy. He allowed himself to feel awkward, declaring himself an ally even before he fully understood the depth of commitment that word represents. He spoke about all of this with breathtaking candor, and it was not only moving, but impactful to others in the virtual meeting, as the word "ally" appeared in his Zoom room. I recall thinking that his company would greatly benefit from the very honest and personal work of reflection he'd done, in a world where reflection is not "actionable." And as he's a leader in pharma, the human ecosystem his company touched would be in better hands. One person, one leader, making this kind of rippling difference.

But because he chose to pause, listen, see, then behave differently, I am certain he will model a level of consciousness and cultural awareness that, from a chief executive, will create new space for people to live and to thrive. I also believe that the life-affirming compounds his company makes, the problems the scientists and physicians are attempting to solve, all will be better served by one leader with the courage to learn, feel, and see.

Chapter 15

Tolls, Toiling, and Tired

Moving down the highways of my life,
making sure I stay to the right . . .
Reading all the signs along the way,
knowing where I am not what they say.

—THE ISLEY BROTHERS,
"THE HIGHWAYS OF MY LIFE"

In a Monday staff meeting, Ron Johnson was more exuberant than usual; he seemed to be moving through the building with even higher-energy voltage than his usual. "This is going to change everything!" he exclaimed, alongside an equally exuberant Catharine Harding, a customer experience research expert. We could now know, quickly and effectively, how customers felt about their experience with us. It was a holy grail level of information that could establish a long and hearty connection with customers. We poured into a room to hear the deep dive of data that would precipitate the Apple Stores' initiating the implementation of the Net Promoter System, a Bain & Company consulting product to assess customer experiences, working closely with Fred Reichheld, the creator of the metrics. Adapting this system was game-changing for us in that it lent accountability to the already high and yet growing expectations of customers. Beyond mere unit sales metrics, these qualitative metrics offer all types of insights to the nonlinear questions every sales organization has. The missing piece for me was, again, how were employees feeling and faring in it all? Again, their perspective was missing from an equation where we relied upon them to run the ball, but we weren't asking them what they needed to do so. It wasn't long before my team had convinced everyone that we needed the same system implemented for our employees. Just as we asked customers, we'd ask our staff the same basic few questions, leading with: "How was this experience?" followed by "Would you recommend working here to friends or family?" And closing with the ultimate "likely to recommend" inquiry that had become the essence of loyalty economics.

Over time, the internal system was also well received, eventually becoming a critical leadership tool. What most of my colleagues did not know was that at early launching, several Black employees reached out to me and asked, "Is this real? Can I really say what I am thinking, and not get into trouble?" With my affirmative response, I watched them breathe some semblance of relief as the more suspect concerns diffused, some requiring more convincing than others. And a few times I could see a perking of curiosity as it sunk in that not only were we asking them their thoughts, but they also might actually matter.

Why did these Black store employees feel the need to ask and be reassured? What about their lives and work experiences had laid the foundation for suspicion? Were other non-Black employees suspect of this new system? Of course. Were the Black staff that had the courage to reach out the only employees with concerns of being identified, tracked, or retaliated against? Surely not. But it was striking to me to receive very similar inquiries from this select group. It was an added toll they had to pay, to assert their need for safety. Cultivating the trust of the nondominant in any organization is core to any hope for thriving. Tuning in to the whispers and acknowledging their right to question their safety is empathy, applied.

Many companies have no high-profile leaders of color as I was at Apple. That was only one of many times I was able to bridge a gap of concern and hopefully engender trust. Even if only symbolically, someone was assuring the intent of integrity. Someone was affirming that the "above and beyond" concerns they carried about that and more, were legitimate and worthy of not being dismissed or ignored. The questioners, their questions, and the past experiences that prompted the questions were real and legit. Validated. Heard and seen. Having underrepresented people sit in decision-making roles who are visible and accessible is essential for companies, or for any roles of public trust. They pay additional tolls and taxes to be there, whether executives are willing to admit it or not. Among other things they are the explainers, question answerers, representatives, quiet mentors, assurers, and decoders. Until there is broader representation inside of companies, the highest level managers or thought leaders who are BIPOC are arguably some of the organization's most precious resources, and they must be cared for and tuned in to accordingly. Even generally, when any organization makes a commitment to be more broadly representative and culturally competent, there is a greater duty of caring, empathy, and compassion to be added to a company's already significant responsibilities. Many will miss the call, even more will dismiss the call. The smartest and best will figure out how to do it, especially as the world changes and demands that we all expand our humanity, requiring more time and more grace.

In 2015, at a gathering for HR professionals, I said to a sizable group of people that diversity training did not work. I knew also that much of that audience would agree with this claim. What I meant was, training had its place of effectiveness, but really only for those who already knew the need, the already familiar and knowledgeable. I knew for years that bias training, formerly known as "sensitivity" training or a few other monikers, went over the heads of most white males. Subject matter that addressed the compounded effects of bias on women and women of color hit invisible walls when it came to the dominant profile. Yet, training was the business solution for the lagging numbers in representation, or for that matter, pretty much any human deficits. Everyone was diversity training their people, however, ad nauseam. The result was that nondominant-profile employees became even savvier about something they already inherently knew. It would be years before the *Harvard Business Review* (the authority to be believed) came out with the study that said diversity training had little effect, especially on male or white employees who hold the most power in the organization. According to this study, no training in use was specifically targeting these power dynamics. So again, DEI teams carried another burden—the failure tax—of the training not being "good enough." The real issue was so much broader and involved, so much more human-centered shifting, and organizations were not ready, willing, or prepared to make the journey.

I know well the added weight of the tolls and taxes of this work, for myself and for countless teams and individuals across commerce. Initially, like many professionals, I absorbed it as *my* failure, but in time I recognized that flawed thinking. "This isn't your harvest," my dad used to say, hearkening back to his rural Louisiana childhood on a farm. He then would add his infamous and always on time "When you find 'em a fool, leave 'em a fool" euphemism and it always made me smile. It was not that people were fools, but that if they were not ready for what you had to say or offer, then went on to dismiss the need for it, according to my dad, that sat them squarely in the "walk away, you don't have time for that" square. The psychological tax, however, still had to be paid; a processing fee, if you will.

At some point I realized, as do so many others, that my personal tolls and taxes had become too expensive, the cost overwhelming any benefit. I needed to start building a path to a post-corporate life, where I could regain myself and my value. I'd often wonder about the extent and complexity of life equations and personal calculus employees were using to evaluate their experiences. I inherently knew it was the organizations that were losing the most.

From time to time I'd have the conversation about tolls and taxes with a couple of trusted colleagues. They'd tell me, "This is what it's like at the top, and you gotta just toughen up. We all have had to." Somehow this felt counterintuitive to me. Why would it not be that at the tops of organizations we'd try to remove barriers to work and barriers to information? Why would those sitting in the most important positions become more closed versus more open? Why become expressionless and less communicative instead of transparent around the intensity and accountability required of us? Did strategy and accountability require us to be less compassionate, less giving? And where fiscal rigor is expected business practice, did generosity of spirit need to be conversely scarce? I refused to believe the two tracks could not coexist. I knew too many people for whom these two philosophies found a home together.

In diversity work, those who tend to be othered, or "excluded," ofttimes work, fight, and demand to be included. The "included" resist; fighting knowingly or unknowingly to maintain their "in-ness." A double penalty is imposed on the excluded. First, you must prove the exclusion is happening, then it becomes your responsibility to fix it. Dr. John Powell would call this "othering." He would also call it trauma. And companies, systems, leaders, decision-makers, power holders, are all astute at "othering" and causing trauma, adding toil, toll, and tax burdens to the very people they invite in to be "included."

Toughen up, suck it up, I was often advised. Listen, what I know about Black women is that toughness is an inherited attribute; we are steeped in resilience, daunted by little. This was not about being tough; this was about being different, thinking differently, feeling differently, and having a different capacity for holding various states of being human. This was a dilemma of carrying a very different kind of intelligence. The kind of intelligence that helped me see and understand why seven decades of the idea of "diversity" had not been realized, why companies were still having the same conversations, poring over the same charts and numbers. The kind of human emotional intel that went unrecognized, and carried a high interest tax rate.

We who are othered have spent years of cycles of examining and critiquing ourselves, doubting, delving, giving in and up. This anguish has driven many diversity practitioners out of companies, and out of the field entirely. It has also decreased the presence of people of color in organizations. At some point people decide to move to a lower cost tax state! I'm taking heart, however, that more of my human work–centered colleagues are starting to say to companies "If you don't get it, you are the problem, not me. I'm not going to waste too much time closing a gap you can't grasp." And they are leaving, moving on to find that place where they are seen. Or, for reasons I completely understand and respect, staying in less tenable or desirable jobs and positions, feeling less fulfilled, striving less and thriving hardly at all, simply finding ways to avoid the burden of added costs to exist.

I have known several women of color who have left important roles as they take the time to address their mental and emotional health before moving on to a new position. One woman I know well has been a senior finance executive at three big companies. She'd said, "I was always given a clue as to where things were headed, when I would begin to be questioned on the two Cs: capability and credibility. Questions that insinuated at my competence. And especially a woman of color in finance, when inquiries that undermine confidence in my abilities or credibility start to rare up, I know it is only a matter of time before a case of concern is leveled against me. I am in cue for a 'no-confidence' designation, and only because I am different, in demeanor and approach." Over the course of her career, she survived countless audits and investigations, and with no gaps of ability or ethics ever formally asserted, she'd simply endured it informally. She'd paid the emotional tax on difference.

Talented, high-potential professionals have internalized messages like this: "It's your fault that you feel this way; you are not [pick one] strong, strategic, ruthless, tough, effective enough." What they hear is "You are not enough." What is really being said is "You are not like us" and "We are not going to adjust to or learn from you; we are the successful and powerful, you adjust to us." For years I observed this affinity bias from the perch of my HR roles and in several companies. In almost every company that I was aware of or knew people within, white men were given significantly more support, coaching, feedback, and space to learn or screw up. To drive toll-free. To enjoy a low or nonexistent emotional tax status. All "others," not so much.

Catalyst, the women's research organization, continues to report that Black women in particular are leaving corporate America. A recent Catalyst study found that 58 percent of Black women reported being "highly on guard" in their workplaces. That's 58 percent of Black women contributing their talent but compromised by justified fear and expectation of being "othered." Denver filmmaker Summer Nettles documents this, directing and producing *She Quit,* a six-episode docuseries about the exodus of Black women from the traditional workforce due to their experiences of health, financial, and emotional trauma.

I had a plan, however. An exit strategy, a life plan I'd been sitting on for some time. I wanted a dog. Space to create, write. As much as I loved the wicked-smart people I worked with, I wanted to choose being around like-minded people who saw the ways we could be world-changing. Of course music would be part of that plan, I'd already started to sing again, and I had become active with SFJAZZ, the premier West Coast presenter of jazz. I'd gotten to know Randall Kline, its founder and executive artistic director. Randall and I had long conversations about experiencing music at the Center, and how critically important it was to attend to everyone's experience with excellence and detail: the artists, audiences, patrons all mattered greatly. It was a shared vision we discovered. He admired my work in the Apple Stores, and that I'd been focused on the very same attributes of experiences. This was a finely tuned way of seeing the world. I was drawn to SFJAZZ for its role in protecting the genre of jazz, but critically important, the idea that Black American music was music that had chronicled the entirety of American history. When SFJAZZ asked me to become a member of their board of trustees, I sensed it would become an important part of my life.

After I joined the board, I actively participated in further diversifying its board and recruiting others. I recall specifically the time scholar and activist Angela Davis and I met in the SFJAZZ offices to discuss her becoming a trustee. Someone took a picture of the two of us, and I sent it to one of my close girlfriends, texting her, "Hey look, here's a photo of me and *the* Angela Davis."

Her response was not what I expected.

She texted back immediately. "Mayday, Mayday, look at you, what is going on with you, sister—you need to figure out an exit strategy now. Things are taking a toll and you've lost the light in your eyes." She made no note of the iconic Ms. Davis in the shot but threw me a lifeline that I did not know I needed and never forgot.

A close friend could see that my vision was blurred and I was weary at a cellular level. And in an errant text in the middle of the afternoon, seeing me, my friend stopped what she was doing, then proceeded to flag me. There are times when the seeing of others is part and parcel of our day, when participating in being present and acknowledging is not difficult or particularly taxing. Then there are moments when we need to register and act. When what you see gives you pause. In that moment, a seed was planted within my psyche by someone I trusted, and I listened. I did not know what to do with it yet, but I heard what she'd said. I'd always been a carrier of light, but it had become dimmer, and she had seen it.

A work trip to Israel opened my eyes to another clue. In my role, it was strategic to be knowledgeable about talent migration patterns across the world and where the most forward technologies were being fostered. Israel, known as a startup nation, was a hotspot of innovation in AI and machine-learning technology. When I returned to the States, I began seeking out the places that could help us succeed in building talent that aligned with what I'd seen there. The recruiting teams were already knowledgeable; I simply wanted to augment our strength, so I had conversations with various schools and centers across the country.

I talked with Cornell Tech, Cornell University's graduate tech program located in Manhattan on Roosevelt Island. The school, which has a partnership with Jacobs Technion Institute in Israel, is known for cultivating and sending future technology leaders and innovators out into the world. I loved what they were doing and how they were going about it, in NYC and on a newly built campus. My mind began to churn, as I knew that several deans of HBCU engineering programs were Cornell grads. Could there be a partnership that benefited all parties? How? With whom? And would this also secure a hub of tech innovators we could leverage? My conversations with Cornell went from introductory to inspirational to transactional to symbiotic.

I was invited to be a guest speaker to a student gathering in summer 2017, and before I even left the campus, they were talking about my joining them there in an executive residency to help redefine inclusivity in the minds of tech creators and leaders. They were not asking me to be their diversity officer! They desired my thought leadership in an area much more impactful.

Clearly this was the beginning of a new era for me. I wasn't certain how or when, but I knew a small part of me had resuscitated. What began as a conversation to tap into their tech intellect in my role as talent chief at Apple led to one of the most fulfilling experiences I'd had in years. More light, more sight. At that moment, I knew I was not as interested in attempting to *fix* from a very distant top as I was motivated to build up from seed stage.

After twenty-one years at Apple, I would "graduate" into contributing to a leading graduate program on a three-year residency. It was the right time, the right duration. It incorporated multiple things I loved. Grad students serious about life and making an impact. New York and the arts community. Time, space, used differently. Being at home and actually being there. It felt perfect. I was thrilled to share my experience and observations of life in Silicon Valley (and, as much as anything else, to share what *not* to do). I wanted to apply the practical lens to the academic environment. But first I had to actually leave Apple.

I was more fortunate than most, however. I'd had years working on a highly regarded mission. I'd had some good bosses, and I'd been promoted at least four times in two decades, culminating in C-suite roles. Yet I too felt the burden of having been othered, being a long-overdue first or lonely only. I'd had seen and unseen experiences. To the extent that my classically trained soprano voice should have been acoustically prominent, it felt subdued. It was a hefty tax and an exhausting toil.

Chapter 16

A Muted Horn Is Still Heard

And keep your hand wide open,
let the sunshine through,
'cause you can never lose a thing
if it belongs to you.

—ABBEY LINCOLN, "THROW IT AWAY"

One Young World is a highly regarded, globally attended conference of young innovators, creators, and leaders, often described as a "junior Davos," where attendees are mentored and counseled for a week by the world's leading thinkers. I was thrilled to have been invited to attend as a counselor for their October 2017 event. I would be on a platform with Kofi Annan, Bob Geldof, and Juan Manuel Santos Calderón, the president of Colombia, since the conference was being held in Bogotá. Serious-minded and intent on addressing real and existential issues, attendees from all over the world, including several Apple employees, would converge in the service of a better and higher vision for the world.

It was also a big deal because it would be my last international trip representing Apple, as I had just recently closed on the agreement with Cornell Tech for an executive residency. I was excited about the trip with this particular organization,

One Young World, and the way they approached mentorship. For a few days it put me in the place I loved being—helping to navigate the future with the best and brightest of tomorrow's leaders.

I'd emphasized to the organizers my desire for a low-key presence with the conference organizers in favor of hands-on interaction with the attendees. They accommodated this without question. All was going well; I was inspired by the attendees, who were global, brilliant, committed, engaged; and the sessions were receiving great feedback. At my third appearance at the conference, I sat on stage for a discussion on how the concept of diversity translated to a global audience. Twelve hundred attendees, significant representation from African and Muslim countries, and women from all around the globe cheered as we talked about being the ones bearing the labels of "diversity" when what we wanted was to be seen, valued, and recognized for our competence. We talked about how the word "diversity" meant so many different things, and we were frankly tired of bearing it. One observer tweeted about me: "She is a BOSS."

At one point, I was asked about my work at Apple and if my diversity work was focusing on the lack of representation of Black women in particular. Here's part of my reply:

I focus on everyone. Diversity is the human experience. I get a little bit frustrated when diversity or the term "diversity" is tagged to the people of color or the women or the LGBT or whatever because that means they're carrying that weight around, and carrying that around on our foreheads. And I've often told people a story— there can be twelve white blue-eyed blond men in a room and they are going to be "diverse" too because they're going to bring a different life experience and life perspective to the conversation. The issue is about representation and mix and bringing all the voices into the room that can contribute to the best product, project, or outcome, of any situation.

After spending the previous evening with Chinese, Swedish, and African nation attendees from more racially homogeneous countries, I was reflecting on the sense that diversity is not just about skin color or gender, but so many deep layers that inform someone's perspective. I was again met with cheers.

Co-panelist and activist DeRay Mckesson, sitting next to me on the stage, quickly qualified my remark with one about white male privilege. (I adored DeRay; we'd already attended several other sessions together.) To clarify the intent of my statement, I assured the audience that my perspective was unequivocally that it was representation that mattered more than the word "diversity" and its stereotypical overuse.

The session closed, and we had a great afternoon, with delegates and attendees closing around to meet me, share contacts, and affirm the morning session's messages. I began the long trip home and settled in. Very soon thereafter began an unraveling of words, time, and space.

The first sign of trouble was from Tim Cook, who was in Europe. He'd forwarded an email he'd gotten from a customer: "Your head of diversity is stupid, and you should do something about her." Confused, I sifted through the email to ascertain she was referencing a quote from the One Young World conference, a quote that extracted part of a comment.

Figuring this was par for the course, I wrote Tim back and assured him it was a positive session and not to fret about this one letter. It would be only minutes before I realized that a TechCrunch article had grabbed the fragmented remarks, sound-bited them, and released them into the social media universe.

The One Young World conference executives reached out to me immediately, assuring me this was a journalistic mishap, not reflective of what had transpired in the room, and not to fret. They would reach out to Tim or whomever else they needed to, including TechCrunch, to tell them the extracted quote was taken out of context and out of sync with the exuberance and affirmation in the room.

I started the early morning in a confident place, quick to dismiss this misrepresentation, but by 10 a.m. I knew. What exactly I knew, I am not sure, as I was still perplexed. I realized I was drinking water nonstop, as though the water would clear things up. I did not realize it at the moment, but I knew this as a singer and performer: when you're about to lose your voice, you begin to uber-hydrate, and you retreat and stay quiet to protect your vocal cords. Your instrument sits deep within your body, and you sometimes feel it before you think.

By this time, it was apparent to me that I was, for the first time in my entire career, in the spotlight of a situation instead of in the background solving (or "Olivia Pope-ing," as many of my staff liked to say) a situation for others as I had done for so many years. My credibility was being attacked, my body of work ignored. My character, belief system, intelligence, motives—all were suspended and subjected to assessment by people I did not know and who did not know me. Blind assumptions were made about who I was and what I stood for.

No one stopped to ask me what I thought; no one stopped to ask me what I meant.

"Welcome to social media," several people said to me. I'll admit, my level of naivete about the up, down, hot, cold, bliss, and brutality of semi-anonymous commentary was pretty high. Prior to this, I'd rarely read comments and had little time or patience to participate in the conversation. But the paralysis this situation invoked was real. It took me back to the playground and Darlita Cross completely miscasting me, my intent, who I was, or what I stood for. Actually, in looking back, Darlita got it and got me a lot quicker than social media did.

I felt disconnected from my body in the strangest way. All the requisite crisis management physiology housed within our bodies took over my command center, all deployed to their respective jobs. Miraculously, so did my own elite team of "special forces." Thanks to my decades of pouring myself into the lives and hearts of others, it all came back to me, in every physical and virtual way, and with attitude.

"Girl, please, we knew what *that* was about."

"Anyone who knows you knew what happened."

"What in the entire _____ did they just do to you??!!"

"You good? We got you, that was some foul s—t, but this is what they do to us, attack the Black women fighting the hardest for the right work!"

"Calling early I know, but needed you to know we have your back, sis."

"Why didn't anyone come to your aid in public? Why didn't Apple? We are pissed to hell at them."

"Uhh . . . I was there in the room and I don't get how that, got to be this."

And on and on. It was as if a death had occurred. Food, flowers, calls, and warnings to stay off of social media, where I was being crucified. I understood that, but like most human beings, I could not stop myself from swiping in, reading a few comments, then retreating. I had not yet taken note of the level of decrescendo in my voice, mostly because everyone else was talking and I was simply trying to breathe.

The first thing I did was reach out to Cornell Tech, as I was set to start my residency there in just a few months. I reached several colleagues and began an explanation, but was stopped short. "A few months ago, we all sat and listened to you address an auditorium full of students," said a key faculty member. "We clearly heard your ideas and values. No one here gave the media blip a second thought, in fact we are even more excited for your arrival." The Dean and Vice Provost added, "These things make academic discourse even more interesting, and more important."

Okay, that was a relief. But why was I still feeling like I was fading, or speaking into a vacuum? Why did I still have such a sense of erasure? I checked in with all the people and places I loved and whose opinion of me I valued. I knew my value proposition as a human being did not rest with the social media public, but I needed more confirmation that the people I did care most about actually saw me, saw through what had happened, with context and perspective. So I ran inventory. Family and loved ones, check. Professional colleagues, check. Truth-Tellers, check. My artist and musician family and colleagues, check. HBCU leaders, check. Trusted Apple colleagues, check. Diversity practitioners from across Silicon Valley, check. Actual conference attendees, check. Coworkers from years prior, check. Cousins I hadn't heard from in years, check. Neighbors, check.

My inventory all came back in the black, no deficits, only one outlier with a slightly stinging critique about what I should have said, followed by what Apple should have said and done, but had failed miserably, in her book. But even these assurances did not override the moments of devastation. Like when *Ebony, The Root,* and other publications dragged me, even though a few years earlier I had been named as one of *Ebony*'s Power 100 in technology, and I was an avid fan and reader of *The Root.*

Michael Harriot, its editor, was a friend of a close college friend of mine. She called him to tell him who I was and who it was *The Root* was actually dragging: a Black woman who was second generation in carrying the torch for representation, an HBCU graduate, still connected to that community and still working on their behalf.

I was indeed a Black woman. Perhaps one too idealistic, one who expected more of others? Should I not have been one who, instead of being called out of my name, canceled, or maligned, called instead into conversation? Why did I not rate as someone to be offered the opportunity to address the alleged transgression? To clarify a statement? It was as if I was told what I had said, forced to choke down the misstatement, sit outside of myself and witness my condemnation, which came in the form of assumptions of incompetence, lack of intellect, or worse, lack of an authentic grasp of what was at stake each day of doing this work and existing as a Black woman in corporate America.

The Black media who took issue with the extracted comments seemed to suddenly not know or remember who I was. Caroline Clarke, a longtime media executive with Black Enterprise, offered clarity. I admired Caroline, had attended several of her annual Women of Power Summits, brought young women leaders with me, and had been named one of Black Enterprise's most powerful women in business in 2017.

· "It will pass," Caroline said. But then, with a long and truthful gaze, "You work for a company that has not been accessible or engaging with our community, regardless of your personal record. So, when there was a chance to drag, it was less about you and more about whom you represented." Indeed, some of the Black media reps I eventually heard from said they participated in the dragging because they believed Apple had not been reasonable with them for ad funding or for leads on Apple stories, seemingly unaware that was not my decision. Others said they were simply doing their jobs, reporting on already reported feeds from other outlets, regardless of what transpired. Most treated it as a blip and suggested I just get over it, all along still treating it as factual.

This was my lesson in twenty-first-century media relations. I took it in, then decided that was enough. I then clicked the life remote. Gathered up the comfiest blankets, the best-smelling candles, registered for VIP DoorDash status, and homed in on my Netflix watchlist. And as self-care and reflection tends to dredge up, insights surfaced. What felt like social betrayal, a collective weapon that silenced me, ultimately became one of my biggest lessons. And though my mom and dad had long since transitioned, I somehow felt them in this life revelation; they had been coauthors of this important story, and I felt their energetic re-engagement.

And that was it: I had a story. A legacy even, but I had

taken a too hands-off approach to it. I had not yet assumed the stance of a fierce protector of it. I had worn it too loosely, assumed it would survive just fine on its own merits. I had been far too liberal in allowing others to contribute their inputs to and versions of it, trusting that any inaccuracies would simply be reconciled by the wise and thoughtful. Just as it had been modeled growing up for those in my era, that in doing the right work, for the right reasons, everything takes care of itself. I now knew, indelibly, the inherent flaws in this logic.

Early in my career, when I was asked about a success formula, I repeated the mantra my father frequently stated: Work hard and smart, do your job well. Competence and confidence will take you where you want to go. This is not just dated advice—it is a flawed theory. Hundreds of years and systems of social constructs do not allow it. Ask any Black woman or man who's deemed successful, and there is a part of our stories that will be consistent. Then it will be followed by the caveats we've all lived. Doing well and working hard does not ensure success, and when you are Black, excellence often garners even more attention—attention that draws ire rather than admiration.

Yet my father, a wise and knowing man, still passed these tenets on to me. I know now they were the colloidal tissue of hope, the psychological infrastructure of resilience. My parents were engaged and deeply invested in an outcome for my life that they believed would surpass theirs. They heeded the advice of teachers and family, doing whatever my first-grade teacher, Miss Lela, told them was necessary to catapult my cognitive success. They immersed me into all things artistic, believing this to be necessary and important guidance as they watched what I paid most attention to in the early years. And they encouraged me to attend an HBCU in the Deep South, absorbing both its academic teaching and its stark life lessons; a plan recommended by beloved uncles and aunts.

I came to realize that in my roles as the seer and advocate of others—coaching, pushing, encouraging, giving—I had taken my own story for granted. I knew the African proverb "Until the lion tells the story, the hunter will always be the hero," yet I had not been a proper griot of my own singular and unique story.

At some point I actually laughed out loud when I realized how today's social media world has manipulated us all to actually not see and not hear one another, literally and figuratively. I laughed out loud, and realized there was no sound. Wait. What just happened to my voice? It was gone. I reached for words, found them, stated them, and nothing came. Did I have a cold? A sore throat? I felt fine. No fever. No cough. Just no voice.

With a scratchy, forced sound I called Patti Andress, my friend, fellow singer, and coproducer. We were soon to start preparing for press and performances introducing my new album. I told her I had no voice. She was quiet. Then she said, "Just rest for a few" but with a knowing tone. She knew. I rested, and still no voice. I tried to speak, sing, no sound. My voice was lost, physically and metaphorically.

In ancient Greece, musicians and physicians were housed together in holy healing shrines, an age-old nod to the healing power of music. There are now apps with the "healing songs" of Africa, Tibetan healing sounds, and Ashanti drum ceremonies. For weeks, I made every attempt to home in on these strategies. I put to work a few of my listening essentials. Dianne Reeves's stirring recording of the classic Milton Nascimento piece "Bridges," Robert Glasper's profound version of Stevie's "Jesus Children of America," Hezekiah Walker's rousing "Power Belongs to God," and Coltrane's "Love Supreme" closed each night. Sounds of Blackness's "I Believe" and Emeli Sandé's voice in "Wonder" awakened me each morning.

I did breathing, exercise, steam. I went to see renowned San Francisco voice physician Dr. Krzysztof Izdebski, who conducted a comprehensive examination. He assured me that I was absolutely fine, with no significant swelling, no nodules, no issues, perfectly healthy.

"I do have some bad news, however," he said. "There is something serious going on in your head and likely your heart, and this must be addressed, because a singer needs these faculties to be able to function." He had really just told me "it" was all in my head!

A couple of months had passed. Sounds were emerging, but I still was not able to speak in my recognized voice or sing at all. I still could not manage a complete vocal phrase. My heart descended to a place I hadn't experienced before, as I tried to imagine any kind of world where I could not sing myself through my days.

Life felt like the end of a record, the needle spinning in perpetuity, no sound emitting but for a few scratches and squeaks; waiting for someone to pick up the needle and flip the record. I quit voice lessons altogether with Carl Franzen, my longtime voice teacher; lessons I had been attending for fifteen years. I stopped rehearsing and cocreating with my favorite collaborator and close friend, Daric Jackson.

While quieted, I spent thoughtful time constructing my departure letter to my Apple colleagues. I was quite ready to pen it. The timing of Cornell Tech's new campus opening had worked out perfectly. The plan was to wind down my work at Apple in the fall, depart during the holiday season, have some downtime, and begin my Cornell residency in the winter term. I leaned heavily into this new endeavor, excited to become bicoastal, traveling monthly to the beautifully designed new campus and a favorite city. But I was not okay.

My voice showed itself just enough to interact with people a few hours a day. But it was not my voice; it was a hoarse, shadowy, gravelly sound that seemed like it came from somewhere other than my body, as if it had emerged from jagged rocks. As frequently as possible I went to visit what was for me a healing space at SFJAZZ, where I could absorb the energy and life force of whoever was on stage. There was always something magical being rendered; Rhiannon Giddens's haunting "At the Purchaser's Option," Lisa Fischer singing Purcell's "Dido's Lament," or Marcus Shelby and Angela Davis telling the stories of women, blues, and Black feminism.

Slowly, something began to resonate. I was responding to the stories the songs told. Dido's fervent plea to be remembered, and Angela's telling of strong women, unseen. The stories were making me hum, stirring me first at a soul level. The stories were relatable; I lost then saw myself in them. Hearing my own voice again after too long a void. I again called on Patti, this time simply in the role of "big sister," and said, "Can we talk?"

We sat at her kitchen table for two nights, eating hummus, drinking tea, and amplifying what the stories were saying to us . . . healing stories, historical stories, stories of our mothers, our life and loves, stories of grieving, stories of having one's voice snatched away.

"No one can actually do that," she said. "You still have your voice, physically or otherwise, and you must decide how you will use it, then coax it lovingly and gently back into service. Give it back its purpose, but not demanding of it the way you were of yourself for years in corporate America. You are not allowed to mistreat it, and that means not allowing anyone to usurp it. It is your divine gift and yours alone. It is there, waiting for you. You are the holdup!" she said in her "I am Glinda, you are Dorothy" way.

I went home and, quietly at first, began to sing. A little each day. It made me smile, and hearing my own voice again started to breathe life back into the spirit that had been weary and damaged. I found stories to sing, I wrote new songs. I sang along to my own yet-to-be-released album. I had not yet set a release date, as I truly feared not ever being able to sing again.

After months of loss, I'd recovered full sound. I'd also begun refilling a reservoir of depletion from years of pouring into others. Years of relinquishing my knowledge to have it too often dismissed or used in the service of something other than affirming life and artistry. I recovered my sense of story. My story. I began seeing again, and giving myself as much as I saw and gave others. I heard my heart speaking again; I heard my son saying new things about life, and I could hear my parents speaking to me in their usual austere, wonderful, and funny ways. I allowed all the stories of my life and legacy to take their rightful places.

When my voice fully returned, I vowed to cherish and steward it, for it was the voice of my ancestors speaking their truth into the future. I was simply a vessel, and my being had declared a pause, allowing me to repair myself. With my newly recovered voice I could now relay my story and be its fierce protector. Because if belonging is nurtured by our seeing of others, sharing our collective stories is the illumination others need, to see one another in mutuality.

Chapter 17

When We See

This light is contagious,
go, go tell your neighbors.
Just reach out and pass it on.

—NAUGHTY BOY, FEATURING
EMELI SANDÉ, "WONDER"

I visited Louisiana for the first time for my great-grandmother Janie Young's funeral in the fall of 1964. Her son, Pete Young, a sharecropper, had died suddenly in his thirties, of unknown causes, when Dad was four years old. My father was nine when his mother also died, from tuberculosis. After this tragedy, my great-grandmother swept up my father and his younger sister and moved them into her farmhouse in West Monroe, Louisiana. Two younger siblings, who'd later manifest to be my beloved Uncle Frank and Aunt Ora, were sent to another relative and raised separately. Somehow, all four remained close in spite of their unthinkable beginning.

To me, Janie Young was a kind, soft-spoken, beloved but somewhat mysterious figure. She was also family legend, fiercely determined, most often seen sporting a crochet shawl and flowered skirts during the week and a decidedly muted, tailored navy blue dress and hat on Sundays. Mama Janie, as we called her, had in her elderly years settled in Colorado with my father and a handful of other close relatives. And from Colorado back to Louisiana she made her final journey . . . in 1964, her body had been transported in a black hearse, by a Black funeral home, back to her home in West Monroe. Dad was determined our family would make it there in time to honor her.

Driving from Colorado to Louisiana may have been an adventure for kid me, but the interstate travel through Arkansas and Texas I now understand was a harrowing trip for my family. We played car games, and I read, snacked, and slept my way through the road trip to the Jim Crow South of Northern Louisiana. Despite their best efforts, in some way I had that cellular level understanding of the trouble we faced as a Black family on the road in the 1960s, and in a shiny white Cadillac no less.

I recall the air standing still when we needed to stop at a gas station, all of us sitting quietly, breath held, to avoid bringing attention to ourselves. I remember the stiff humidity in Texas, and the slow, lumbering, unpleasant gas station attendants. I remember vigilance. And to this day, I recognize that same sense of vigilance for my son, every son, for every Black child, man, woman, for anyone Black, brown. We stay vigilant, always.

We did make it to Louisiana and spent several days there. One day, after Mama Janie was buried, my two cousins and I decided we wanted to go to a matinee movie. My cousins were confident and excited to host me in the familiar (segregated) parts of the small town, where everyone knew them and the family. We arrived at the theater and paid for our tickets. I charged straight ahead toward the main doors, until I felt my cousin's hand grab my jacket, forcefully pulling me back.

"What?" I asked my older cousin, Ronnie. He turned to his younger brother with a "you tell her" kind of look. My younger cousin, Jerome, was affable and fun and had a great way with words.

"Ummm . . . that's not our door, Cuz," he said. "We have to go in that way," pointing upward.

"But I like to sit in the front!" I said. "So let's hurry before the movie starts," and off I went. Again the stern voice and look from Ronnie, and a less affable explanation.

"Denise Sharlene! We are not allowed to go in that door, and we are not allowed to sit on the first floor, and you are going to get us in big trouble," he said.

"We *get* to sit in the balcony!" Jerome said with a hopeful grin.

"But I don't *like* the balcony!" I said. I pouted but proceeded to follow them upstairs to the obviously low maintained area with a musty wood smell. And I sat down to watch the movie in the Colored Balcony section of the movie theater in West Monroe; fuming, for reasons I did not entirely yet understand at nine years old.

For the first time in my young life, I realized the pre-movie news clips, the concessions, the entire experience was not intended for me, for us. It was a powerful "othering" experience. I, we, were made to feel barely tolerated. By no means was this movie house intended to entertain people who looked like us, and that exclusivity was made profoundly clear and obvious. The heaviness of that reality took my breath away and weighed down my spirit. I felt something dark and sad from that moment, and its deep violet-to-black hue has stayed connected to that memory.

I noticed other little things that gave me that same feeling, such as the way people (white people) stared at us in our car, or the snail pace of the man selling ice cream cones to ask what flavor we wanted, obvious that he did not really want us to have any ice cream whatsoever. I believed this heaviness existed just in the small towns in Louisiana, so I tried hard to disassociate the eeriness of it from the rest of my life experiences. The "Colored" signs, the ways in which the supposedly no longer segregated town managed still to separate Black and white in orderly and definitive ways. The ways in which our every move was vigilant and focused. I have never nor will I ever forget it.

This was my childhood introduction to the segregated South, the aftermath of Jim Crow, which was the aftermath of Black Codes, which was the aftermath of a country at war over enslavement ideology and enslavement economics, followed by reluctant and resentful emancipation; all within the arc of the systemic oppression that continues to this day. To make it clearer, my grandfather Pete Young was a sharecropper, and sharecropping was the economic replacement of enslavement. Only three generations before me, my family would have been owned. And though my experiences were different from my parents', I had been prepared and seasoned by their imprinted memories. I am generationally only a moment, a glimpse away from this time, a time I can still feel in a moment's memory many decades later.

The power of one's environment is undeniable. Who and what we are surrounded with informs who we will become, overlaying experiences onto our natural, yet perhaps undeveloped or even undiscovered gifts. I am not sure how fully mindful my parents were of this; they just lived it. They were, as I would turn out to be years later, strong believers in the power of experiences. They were generous in the variety and diversity of people they brought into our home and our lives. They were undaunted by cultural differences, and socially inclusive if you were good and trustworthy, their absolute litmus test. They were protective, cautious, and spent lots of time talking to each other and other relatives about how I would be raised.

My parent's deliberate, determined care and vigilance are traceable in every phase of my life. Every action was a lesson of sorts, like how my mom would snap, "Get out of my kitchen," when I would try to hang out in ours. Large, with lots of deep rich wood and golden hues, our kitchen was a warm and inviting place to be in our house. My mother was an incredible cook, and I would poke around to try to understand how and what she was cooking. She was persistent in booting me out.

"What's that on the stove?" I would ask.

"Find out when I call you; now go do your homework."

"It's finished already."

"Then go read a book."

"I already read all my library books."

"Then go read your encyclopedias and come back with something new you've learned." Sigh. I'd return to my room and find something entertaining until I was called for dinner or to set the table. Years later I would finally understand why she never wanted me there. She'd say my studies were more important, and she wasn't keen on me, as a woman, being more known for cooking than intelligence, or even the idea of garnering the attention of some unsuspecting fellow with skillful cooking, apparently a thing that could happen. (This turned out never to be an issue.)

Their generation was conditioned to believe that as a woman, if you were educated and hardworking, this would serve in securing you a good and independent life. They did not want to risk my becoming "domestic" in any way, including by profession, even though one might assume that era had long passed. It had not. A close great-aunt had been, even in my childhood years, a "domestic" for a white family in the Broadmoor area of Colorado Springs. She was "the help." She drove up in a fabulous red Buick, entering through a separate door. She changed from a well-appointed dress into a sparkling white uniform. She was not "staff"; she was their cook. An exquisite and elegant one, but a cook, for hire, by a white family. My parents were imprinted by the fact that several brilliant women they knew, with many types of talents, were severely limited by a racially charged world. A mean and unforgiving world that dictated that talented Black women could still fall victim to a tragic life, unless they were educated, hardworking, focused in specific professions, and determined.

The whole of my environment included the proverbial village of people dedicated to my belonging and my success: aunts, uncles, cousins, church, teachers, community. I'm certain several of them didn't see the time and effort they spent with me as a long-term success strategy; they simply wanted to make sure I was safe, educated, and balanced. For my parents, who grew up in the Jim Crow South and the tough streets of Brooklyn, safe, educated, and balanced equated to resounding success. They already knew I would have compassion, that I had the extra ability to see and care; that was both my nature and their nurturing. They never foresaw the arc of where I would ascend, but their vision for me was what kept me grounded in my life, my community, my roots, yet still able to see a big picture, ofttimes seeing what others did not yet.

In turn, I tried doing the same for my son, Ian. Ian was not a difficult child to raise, but he was always a challenge because his creative talent and intellect just did not manifest typically. He was a toddler with very old-soul concerns, obedient while testing every edict. He noticed everything, taking it all in. I'd apparently passed onto him some of the same things I loved. Music, art, dance. He saw them from completely different angles, though, seeing the intricacies of how movies were made, how letters were formed, how design elements told a story. His math paper margins were spectacular and ornate, while the teacher incongruently issued a C+ grade at the top of the paper. What could a grade possibly say about the mind of the child who'd created da Vinci–quality borders for his fractions assignment?

"It's all in the hands," Ian's father said when he first laid eyes on him. "His hands are long and will be conduits for everything he sees in life." An artist and pianist himself, Daniel saw Ian profoundly, even when I did less so, or when I focused too intently on controlling outcomes.

My father also saw him. "No spankings or punishments for this one," he said. "He won't understand; he needs to know the reason behind things. That talent he has makes it harder; you're going to have to talk him through a lot of things he'll need to understand about this world."

Dad taught Ian how to save money (a lesson I'd been taught decades earlier). He talked to him about working for himself, and about protecting his "jewels" (Dad's version of the birds and bees). He talked to him about anger management many times over the years, starting from when Ian was only five. It was as if he knew this had to become a lifelong skill to address a centuries-long struggle, and he wanted to mitigate it as a major distraction as much as possible, and as soon as possible.

One story I recall vividly hearing him share with Ian was when Dad was assigned to a U.S. Navy hospital ship where he served in WWII. (That mere fact in and of itself was historical, given the known segration policies of the U.S. Navy.) After a brief and trivial disagreement, Dad was spat upon by a peer, a white sailor. My father described going blank, then dark with rage. He could not see, he said, he was so angry. As enraged as he was, in that moment he told Ian he assessed everything, all that was or would be at risk: his entire life, his future, the lives of everyone who'd endured all they'd endured to see him through life and onto this navy vessel. In one instant, he knew it could all be destroyed.

"I held my peace," he told my son. "I prayed to God, and I held my peace, and I did it for you, not even knowing there would be a you, but I knew with one wrong move, I would lose my life, my freedom. In that moment I learned that anger can be death, and I chose to live, and now you must understand that choice."

Like every mother, I believed my job was to prepare my child for life, but I also prioritized empathy, compassion, and seeing the perspectives of others. I didn't realize then that those traits were already built into Ian. We had a tradition of spending every Martin Luther King Jr. holiday going to a theater or renting a movie: *Cry Freedom, Mississippi Burning, Schindler's List, Malcolm X*. Every Mandela film. As my father had advised, I tried to connect dots and explain everything to him. I was unable to replicate the dinner table lesson teachings my parents had offered me, so I did the best I could, in whatever formats I could secure.

We went to countless music performances, from symphonies to plays to concerts, all of which were accompanied by a discussion or a recording. We saw a classic live performance of tap dancers Gregory Hines, Fayard Nicholas, and Honi Coles, where I insisted he see the origin of the beat, moves, and syncopation of the breakdancing he dearly loved at that time. I was unrelenting with the life lessons, and it was likely pretty exhausting for Ian, but he managed through it.

I had raised a seeing, hearing, feeling son, one who had arrived here with these traits in tow; I just stewarded them along. Once off to art school in Southern California, in the spirit of compassion for me, Ian decided to no longer inform me of all the times he was pulled over, profiled, and harassed. We'd had "the talk" when he was old enough to ride a bicycle to school, around age nine. Even there in Colorado Springs, where his grandfather was in public office, we pleaded and preached the "you must survive the stop" gospel.

As his mom, I'd seen much in Ian—his artistic gifts, his sense of faith and compassion. What I missed was the extreme depth of his capacity to love, and therefore to be hurt. When we lost several family members closely in a row—his father, Daniel; my father, who was also Ian's profoundly loved grandfather; my mother, Claudia, whom he adored as I did; and others, Ian almost did not survive it. The losses were too much, and he sank into a period of depression and alcohol abuse. A lengthy and difficult season followed. With years of work, courage, and prayer, we made it through, with both of us on a long journey of healing and recovering. These days we spend a lot of time together and practice seeing each other, calling things out as we see them, as a matter of ritual. It is our sport, our outlet to help one another manage the fact that we both see so much, and as two very like beings, grieve it all immensely.

For those of us in this world who do see and feel deeply, the burden can be overwhelming. We yearn to share the responsibility, to simply make human connection a conscious choice, one we all could make more space for in our lives, because truly it only requires moments. People like Ian and myself need others to share in this. We wish daily for it.

Chapter 18

Meeting Ourselves Where We Are

When you see me like this,
and when I see you like that,
then we see what we want to see . . .

—CÉLINE DION,
"IT'S ALL COMING BACK TO ME NOW"

As a storyteller I am an advocate of gathering our life stories. Gathering the memories, the people, the moments, and sitting with them just long enough to see how they shaped us. The result of even minimal reflection can be revelatory. It can help us see how we touch and impact everyone else in our path. It can illuminate some of the mystery we claim not to understand about ourselves. It's all there. There were people who helped, people who hurt, people who saw us. Words mattered. Most of us are aware and smart enough to learn from this reflection, and make decisions about what we'd like to carry forward in life. Or, we need to bounce if off of someone, a friend or even a professional. I was fortunate to have people in my life who were both friends and professionals at helping others navigate the hard and difficult stuff, the stuff we all carry. I spent time doing the kind of work that most people don't believe in; the kind that facilitates fundamentally better mental health and clarity. I'm not embarrassed or shy about having done a lot of "the work," and will still do so, as long as life is as complex as it is, presenting head-scratching challenges daily. Everyone needs a way to maintain every dimension of ourselves, every gift deserves our care.

At some point I realized the seeing of others was indeed a gift. I did not always own it, did not always know I was doing it. I now recognize it readily when I see it in action, in myself and others, and it is a pretty spectacularly powerful force we have as humans. When we dismiss it we leave voids that could have altered a moment, or a life. We pass, we ignore, we don't have the time. That actually is okay if, when a very obvious opportunity sits in front of you, you allow yourself to act on it. Small, large, insignificant, privately, it doesn't matter. Steve Jobs famously said that Apple attracted anyone "who really wants to get in a little over their head and make a little dent in the universe." What if, in a complex and chaotic world, a version of "getting in a little over our heads" is really digging in a little deeper into how we can see others? Which others do we decide we will *see,* and why?

Can today's version of Steve's "a little over our heads" mean the unlearning of what we now know is untenable or even unjust in how it affects others? Could relearning be that we no longer respond to unfounded fear or discomfort about others?

The imbalances of these times might need us to be more connected versus isolated, where we can gather more equilibrium. More aligned than polarized, to get more done. Calmer versus anxious. More surprise moments of humanity when someone simply comes through. When we are seen, light is cast onto something formerly dimmed or darkened. Something forgotten, something I did not expect you to notice.

What if "a little over our heads" meant something so simple as pausing just long enough? Long enough to offer hope, ask a question, take note. At scale, an individual pause to see can translate into an entire movement to include. Fortune 500 companies, with their $37 trillion in market value and the twenty-nine million people employed by them, could, by sheer force of numbers, shift the course of the world. But only if they also shift their consciousness in the very same ways can they pivot their business direction and invest in their futures.

Whether aware of it or not, modern commerce has within its virtual walls the necessary attributes for both social engineering *and* economic transformation. Business leaders will claim they do not, that the two cannot coexist, or that they have no need to do so—or interest in doing so. It is, again, safer for some in business to relinquish accountability to institutional investors, shareholders, etc.; concepts much of the world does not understand. Yet the business community has within its grasp a "solve" it is tardy to embrace. But it must. The leaders of tomorrow—many of the ones I talk to week to week—see hope in these revolutionary moments in time. There are many willing to shift, learn, and unlearn. They understand the why; they feel, care, and see.

It is said that the need to belong is a part of the human genome. Tribal Africa held complex patterns of acceptance, ways of seeing one another, roles for fostering meaning to the tribe. Being seen is the kinetic force behind human connection. It endorses our existence to others and, most crucially, to ourselves. It is both physiological and emotional, as documented biologically through the release of oxytocin when we feel accepted. It holds unbelievable power that has the potential to change the direction of a life ... our own or someone else's.

For those of us who hold membership in various marginalized groups—whether race, gender, identity, ability, appearance, or so many more—the opposite of being seen is something we have experienced in abundance: from forcible and brutal oppression to the organic weightiness of being overlooked, brushed aside, unheard, or dismissed. It chips away at our ability to connect with others in our work, in our lives, and toward our purpose. When we are unseen humanly and systematically it's even harder to connect with the mission of a community or enterprise, and we are expected to do so without question or even discussion. As much as we may try, the toil and tax of it is humanly untenable. We disengage, become dispirited, disenfranchised, and we do so often profoundly unaware of how affected we truly are, how devastated our souls are.

When the Colombia incident faded, and with it the drama and speculation over "what really happened," I was excited about pretty much everything. I was producing and premiering a children's opera, establishing a long-wished-for bicoastal lifestyle, and finalizing my album release under my own production company. And at the end of a year-long wait list, I'd flown to Colorado to bring home the newest family member, my Bernedoodle puppy, Blakey, named after the great jazz drummer and band leader Art Blakey. Puppy Blakey was my own little messenger, reminding me that life's basics, such as a bacon chewy biscuit and running like blazes after absolutely nothing, were essential to a having a good day. Blakey was joined by a second puppy, Bella, contributing more life lessons and training for me, not for her.

My Cornell residency completed, in the summer of 2020 I began serving as the chair of the board of SFJAZZ, still one of my places of restoration. A premier arts organization thanks to a visionary founder, they are at a critical inflection point as they continue to elevate Black American music to its rightful place as a chronicling of America's story, the full truth of it. Terence Blanchard, Wynton Marsalis, Terri Lyne Carrington, Jason Moran, Dee Dee Bridgewater, Darin Atwater, and so many more musical giants who are now leading major organizations can and will be a force against erasure, as music serves as an impenetrable container for a thriving existence in this world. I feel well placed to assist with its uplifting to where it remains as important and is seen as the powerful unifying musical language it is.

I am a director for the amazing designer and retailer Thom Browne, another founder of a creative movement, one that understands how to include through design, enveloping us in brilliance and wit, all while allowing us to be uniquely ourselves within it.

I have one staff member and two artists under Blue Organza Productions, and my recording studio is built and operative. I am excited that it will serve as a container and vessel for more stories and more voices.

I have received four honorary doctor of humane letters degrees, the first from my beloved alma mater, Grambling State University, and the most recent from Colorado College, in my hometown. It was my son, Ian, who took pause with me when hearing me say one day, "But I didn't really earn those degrees." Usually it's me lecturing him about owning all aspects of his story, but this time I was the on the receiving end of the lesson. "Four important universities recognized your work in this world, Mom, so maybe it is time you do too?"

Five years ago I left Apple. I haven't been inside of day-to-day operations of a massive corporate environment since then, but my work in inclusive culture creation is far from done. I am in frequent close contact with people reaching out to me from major companies; from the amazing Stacey Blissett, one of the Apple Stores' first Black female geniuses I am still in contact with, to senior executives sitting in various roles and situations, I am always willing to hear and help as they ascend or face turning points. I do my best to help them navigate scenarios I hoped we'd be long past, yet here we are. I will not abandon them, and I am inspired by their perseverance. Imparting much of what I have written in this book, their feedback has been significant enough to affirm my reasons for writing it.

As much as it has been a matter of my life's course, I must acknowledge the significance of having been a "first" and an "only," especially in an otherwise progressive industry. Too many women and people of color are still today having to forge paths in technology and other industries, making it important that they hear from me, and from others like me, like us. We live in an era where stories like mine are readily minimized, if told or allowed to be told at all. We live in an era of casual erasure. Books banned, missing eras, superficially told digital stories, AI bias infiltration. History is not being revisited or revised, but rewritten. And my journey, my presence was felt and seen by millions, and simply should not be erased.

See me; because in doing so, you see so much more, so many more.

My story highlights why our seeing others matters deeply, and why representation matters profoundly. We all have an opportunity to impact the culture around us and not wait for a diversity officer, a supervisor, a CEO, a PTA president, or a political figure to do so. Through reading my stories, you may choose to see how your own stories are sources of strength and power, and you may be less inclined to underplay the moments that changed your life or gave you life. Knowledge of our own lives and what ignited us helps us recognize when we see the same opportunity for others. We have power. Power to shift consciousness, culture, even behavior. The moments when we think we are without power are the moments we have it and in abundance. In those moments there is a patience to have new discussions, and that is powerful. In those moments we find new courage and figure out new ways and reasons to talk to each other. That is power. In those moments it is important to not feel helpless, but to know we hold the agency to do more. Not succumbing to helplessness is powerful. Hopefully we now see more clearly all that is at stake if we were to take no note or no action whatsoever about what we can do. Some of us are refusing to be complicit by not allowing others to continue evading accountability. Some of us are vowing to see and hear more around us. Many of us have redefined what *essential* looks like, and we make a choice to respect those who truly are essential, no longer ignoring or dismissing their humanity. We are being more honest about how much we will tolerate from systems that have never served us in the ways they claimed to. We are changing our relationships with technology and with one another. We have looked around us and begun to note that loneliness and isolation is, indeed, an epidemic, as Surgeon General Vivek Murthy's 2023 study has warned.

The places and spaces where we all work and carry out an extended version of our lives can also become a collective force of change. Not the entities, Inc.s, structures, or buildings where we work. Not the groups, teams, trucks, cubicles, stores, hospitals, departments, schools where you find us all neatly categorized and counted . . . but the *us* inside of them all. The essence, the real force . . . is us.

We can choose to create our own ecosystems of inclusivity, connection, and progress. We don't have to wait for long-awaited legislation, for disconnected, disparate, unfair systems to right themselves, for tribal leadership to suddenly become caring and communal, or for billionaires to return from space. We don't have to await the appointment of a "diversity" person, and we don't have to be trained on how to learn about the lives of others. Small children do it every day. We only have to care. Sight will follow.

Notes

Chapter 3

27 As W. E. B. Du Bois wrote—Du Bois, W. E. B. *The Souls of Black Folk*. Chicago: A. C. McClurg & Co., 1903.

27 Today, 107 HBCUs—Parker, Virgil. "A Guide to America's Historically Black Colleges and Universities," The Aspen Institute, September 15, 2020. https://www.aspeninstitute.org/blog-posts/what-you-should-know-about-historically-black-colleges-and-universities/#:~:text=While%20the%20nation's%20107%20HBCUs,%25%20smaller%20than%20non%2DHBCUs.

27 A McKinsey Global Institute Study—Bevins, Frankki, Kathryn Fox, and Duwain Pinder. "How HBCUs Can Accelerate Black Economic Mobility." McKinsey & Company, July 30, 2021. https://www.mckinsey.com/industries/education/our-insights/how-hbcus-can-accelerate-black-economic-mobility.

33 Their research showed—Duhigg, Charles. "What Google Learned From Its Quest to Build the Perfect Team." *The New York Times,* February 25, 2016. https://www.nytimes.com/2016

/02/28/magazine/what-google-learned-from-its-quest-to-build-the-perfect-team.html.

34 40 percent of all Black engineers—Bevins, Frankki, Kathryn Fox, and Duwain Pinder. "How HBCUs Can Accelerate Black Economic Mobility." McKinsey & Company, July 30, 2021. https://www.mckinsey.com/industries/education/our-insights/how-hbcus-can-accelerate-black-economic-mobility.

Chapter 6

63 "I wish I could say"—"I Wish I Knew How It Would Feel to Be Free," music by Billy Taylor, lyrics by Dick Dallas.

Chapter 8

94 "For you I have written a song"—"Fly Me to the Moon," music and lyrics by Bart Howard.

Chapter 10

145 Jodi Halpern has been—Halpern, Jodi. "Research." Jodi Halpern, March 24, 2023. https://www.jodihalpern.com/research/.

Chapter 14

194 The stories and laments—Cutter, Chip, and Lauren Weber. "Demand for Chief Diversity Officers Is High. So Is Turnover." *The Wall Street Journal,* July 13, 2020. https://www.wsj.com/articles/demand-for-chief-diversity-officers-is-high-so-is-turnover-11594638000.

Chapter 18

249 "When you see me like this"—"It's All Coming Back to Me Now," music and lyrics by Jim Steinman.

251 Fortune 500 companies, with their $37 trillion—"Fortune Announces 2022 Fortune 500 List." *Fortune* Media, May 23, 2022. https://www.prnewswire.com/news-releases/fortune-announces-2022-fortune-500-list-301552608.html.

Acknowledgments

The idea of sharing one's story is a very natural thing for me. For others. When it was first raised to me to consider sharing my own story, it took some coaxing. My reluctance was not from some false sense of humility, but what was my message? I am not "memoir" famous, only business-distinction worthy. Is that a book? What did I want to say? Who did I want to say it to, and did I feel absolutely compelled that I needed to say it?

I remember thinking it might translate into a nice lengthy article, but I did not foresee the volume and velocity of information my memory hard drives had stored up. It had not yet fully registered that in my life I'd covered a lot of ground. The globe. Events, eras, and seasons. My friend Seth Goldenberg, a radically curious seer himself, introduced me to David Drake, head of Crown Publishing. The three of us sat together and riffed creative. By the end of that meeting, I was convinced that this, indeed, was a story I had to tell, that I had a responsibility to tell. I had a responsibility to cast light upon what it is like to be a first, and only, one of few.

I had a responsibility to do so having worked in an industry notorious for its absence of stories from people of color, and a Black woman's perspective that spanned over two decades had to hold some insights. Who might care about those insights? Anyone at all who traveled a path of not feeling seen in their work, profession, or life. And anyone who had been seen in some special way that had propelled them into the universe on an unexpected path. That turns out to be a hell of a lot of people. This book also carries a strong theme of mutuality. Life is not one-way. As we are seen, so can we "see" others, and the proven physiological, emotional, and psychological impact of what can happen when we're seen is so humanly profound it almost defies quantification. We can be more deliberate about remembering when we were seen, and how it altered our lives. And we can be more intentional about the seeing of others, bolstered by the knowledge that doing so holds a kind of power we feel, recognize, but do not always take the time to understand, as it is sometimes bigger than ovur understanding.

I would like to take time to acknowledge and see all those who sat on either side of this equation for me.

Thank you to Kathleen Murray Harris, who miraculously sorted out six decades of raw assets to come up with an infrastructure for how this story could unfold. I refuse to remove our weekly time slot from my iCal, and I remain impressed by her Word dexterity, thankfully making up for my lack thereof. We did great work!

Thank you to Libby Burton for the initial attraction to my story, for the patience, and for helping me to shape it with a poet's sensibility and extraordinary editing intelligence. You got it, you got me. I was seen.

Thank you to a very long list of important life "seers" comprised of close family, teachers, and earliest seers. I learned how to navigate my path through you. If you thought I wasn't listening, I was. If you thought I did not hear you, I did. If you thought I was just passing through, I retained everything and more you hoped to impart.

Some of you are named in the body of the book, many are not. I wish I could circle back to every single one of you to thank you for what you did for me. I will list several: Dad, Mom, Uncle Frank, Aunt Ora, Cousin Jim, Cousins Jerome and Ronnie, Uncles Ray, Jim, and Bill. Monclova Photography in Brooklyn. Aunt Ruth, Uncle Peter, Aunt Helen. The Young family of Calhoun and West Monroe, Louisiana. The faculty, then and now, at Grambling State University. The family of Daniel Haynes. The Smith family. Claudia. Fran. The Jacksons. Ivan. Tammie. The Foster family. My Apple family, alumni and those still denting the universe, thinking differently, and leaving the world better. And to all of those who allowed me to share with you how I saw you, I hope you now or will soon understand the importance of those moments.

Thanks to Keith Yamashita for holding an image of me that he saw, then saving it for when I could see it. Thanks to Patti, Tuck, and Carl for sending lifelines to my voice; pulling it out of peril and playing it back to me. Thanks to Nancy, Roland, and Kathy for the journeys that kept me sorted, sane, and discerning. Thanks to my ride or dies, my great friendships, sisterhoods, sorors, fellow artists, advocates, musicians, and storytellers. Thank you for riding and for believing we'd all survive the process.

A special thank-you to my bonus family: Gina, Gael, Juliann, Pierre, Bronson, Koleman, and Gwen. Ours is a collective story worthy of note, yet unfolding. We will see it through.

Finally, thank you to Ian. I have been in awe of you from the very moment you arrived, looking very much like you were already in progress on your own mission of seeing. I could not be more thrilled in this lifetime to have been upheld, inspired, and seen as you have seen me—faithfully, with utmost honesty, always hopefully.

About the Author

Denise Young recently closed a brilliant two-plus-decades career as a cocreator of Apple's retail store experience, ascending to VP level under Steve Jobs and as the first African American to rise to C-level at the company, reporting to CEO Tim Cook as the worldwide HR Chief, and the company's first VP of Inclusion and Diversity. Post Apple, Denise served as the second Executive in Residence at Cornell Tech, advising new and future tech leaders of the importance of humanity and digital inclusion. She advises HBCUs, arts organizations, academic institutions, and individual leaders on talent and culture. Denise currently serves as board chairperson of SFJAZZ, the premier arts-presenting organization in San Francisco, boasting a global membership and the only free-standing building in the world to exclusively serve jazz. A director/trustee for designer Thom Browne and a vocal artist, writer, and producer herself, Denise espouses the concept her former CEO Steve Jobs spoke about, that it is the intersecting of technology, humanities, and the arts that makes the heart sing. A 2022 recipient of the American Composer Orchestra's Creative Catalyst Award alongside composer John Adams, Denise has been named a "Most Powerful Woman" by *Ebony* and Black Enterprise, named one of the "100 Most Influential in Silicon Valley" by *Business Insider,* and was featured in *Fortune*'s "Most Powerful Women" issue.